"A Surrealistic Journey"

Grayscale Coloring Book

"A Surrealistic Journey"

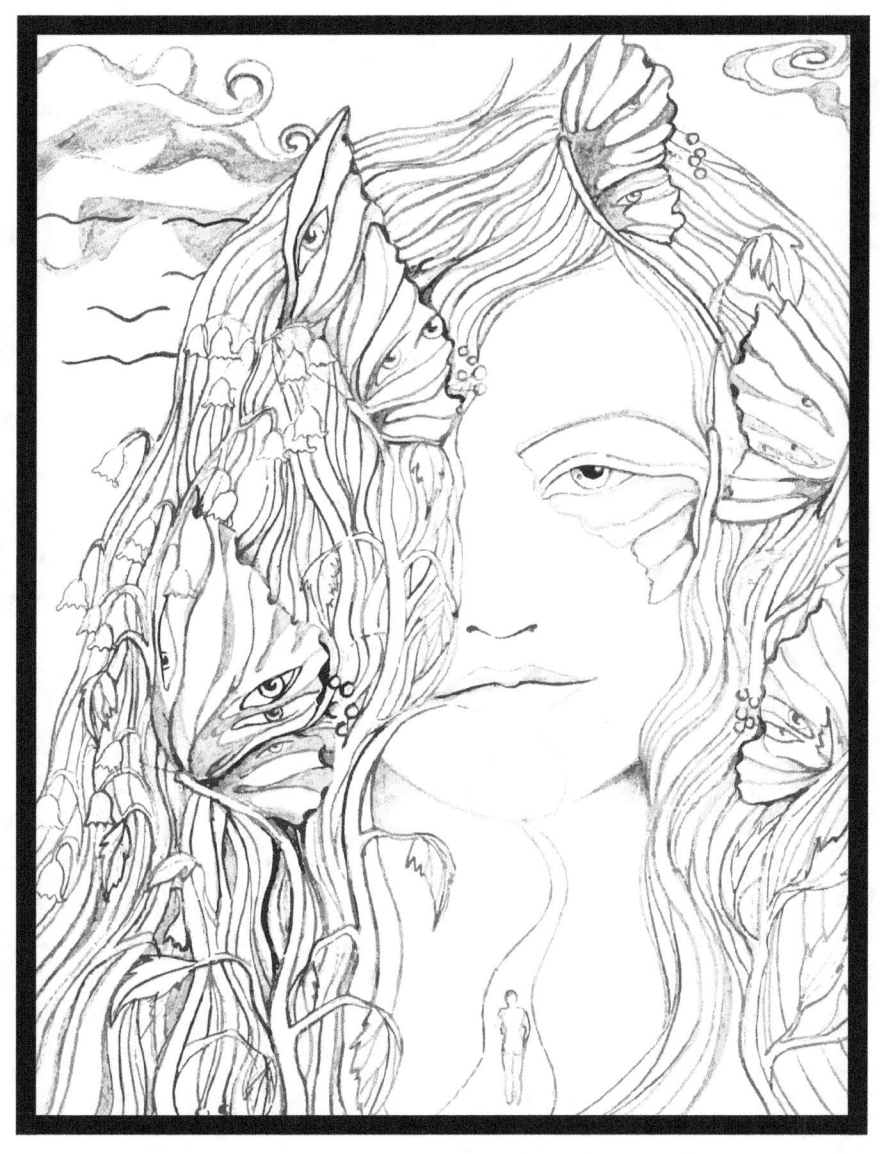

Grayscale Coloring Book

Serena Daugette

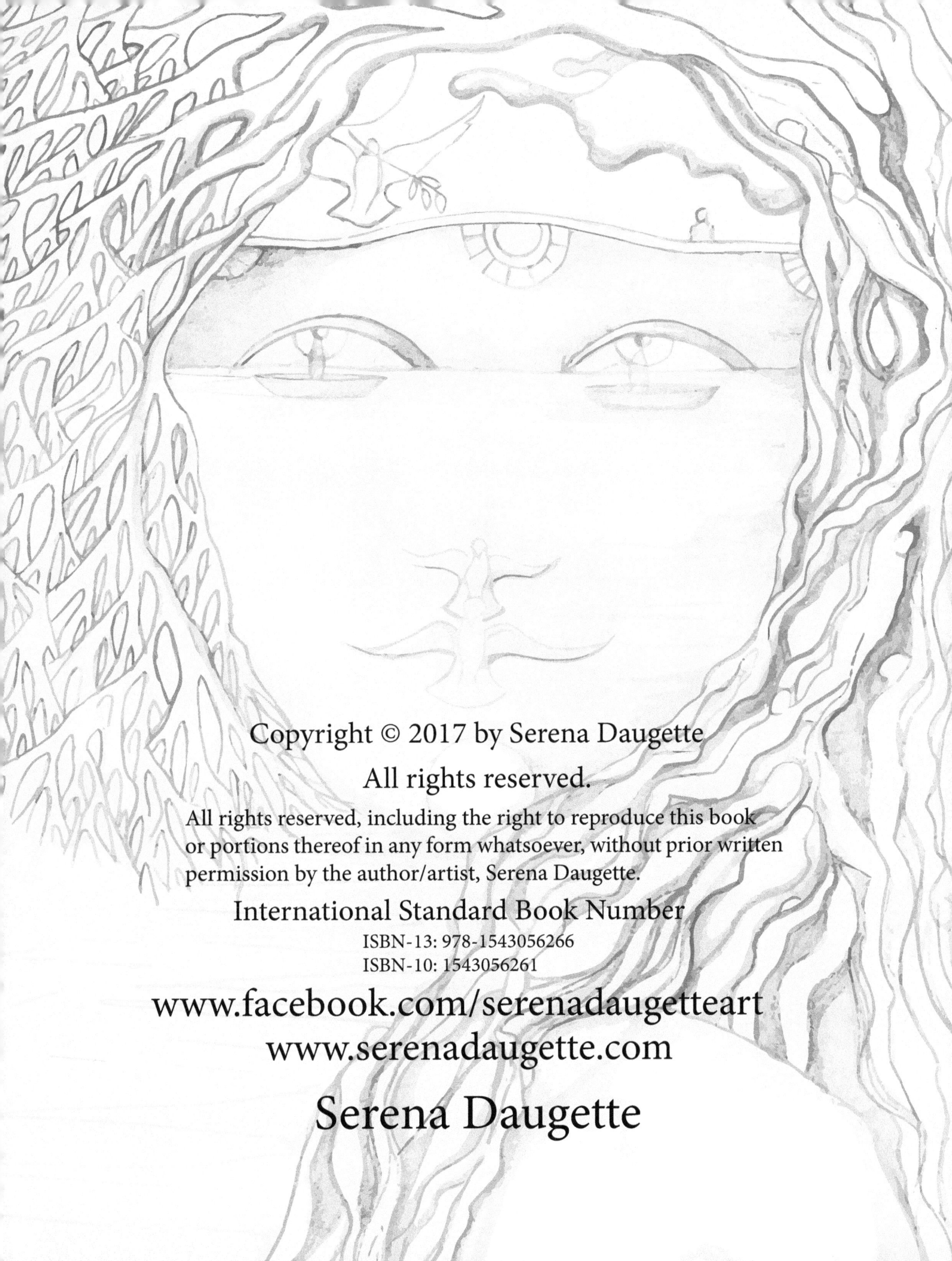

International Standard Book Number
ISBN-13: 978-1543056266
ISBN-10: 1543056261

www.facebook.com/serenadaugetteart
www.serenadaugette.com

Serena Daugette

This book is dedicated in memory of my brother, Harol Daugette. Thank you for all the love, support, and humor you brought into my life. I'm so grateful to have had you.

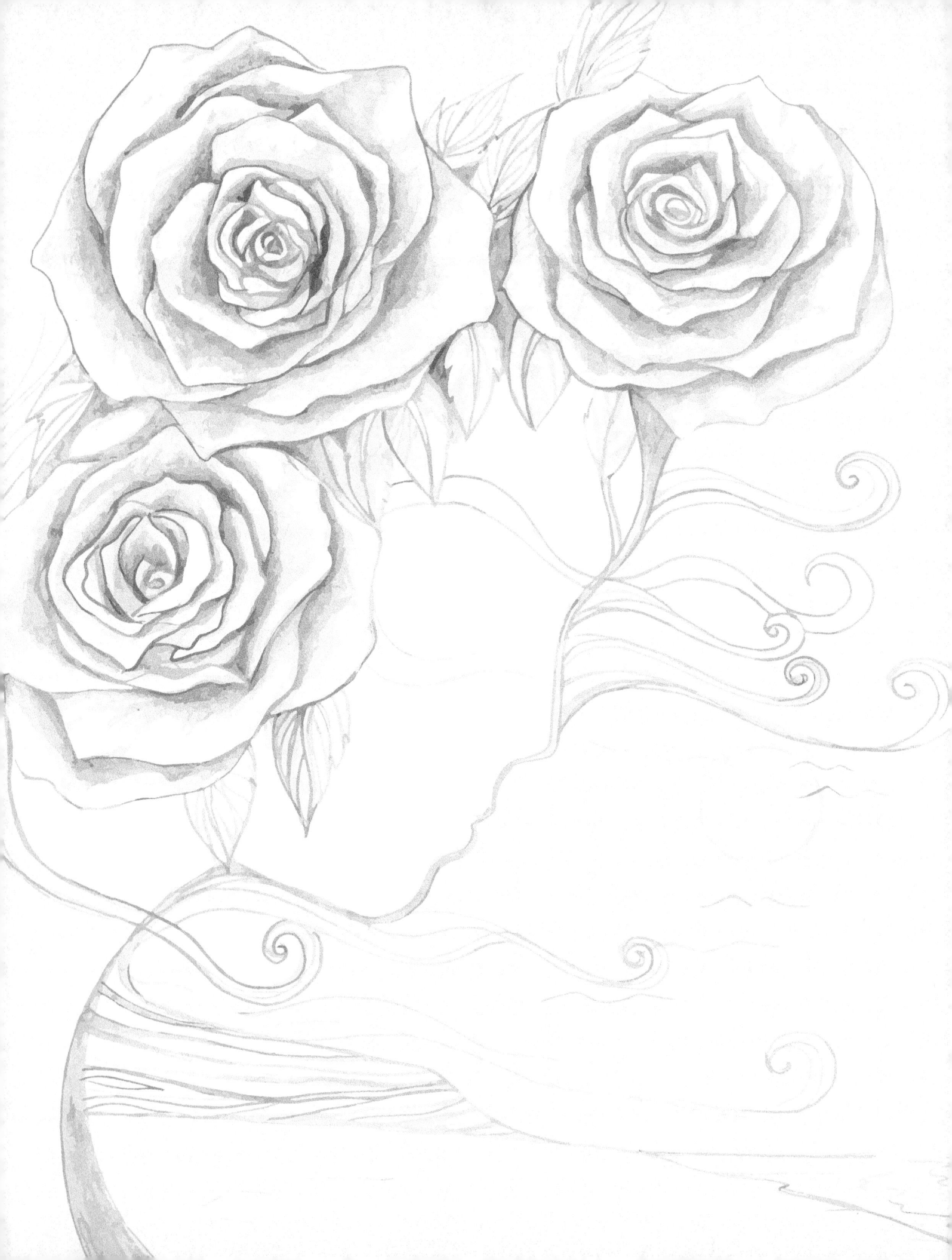

There was once a young girl who dreamed of traveling to a far away land. She dreamed of seeing all the beautiful places in the world. She dreamed of the wind taking her where she should go. As she looked up from the canopy of the tree she saw a beautiful feather floating by and at once a voice telling her to follow and so, she did...

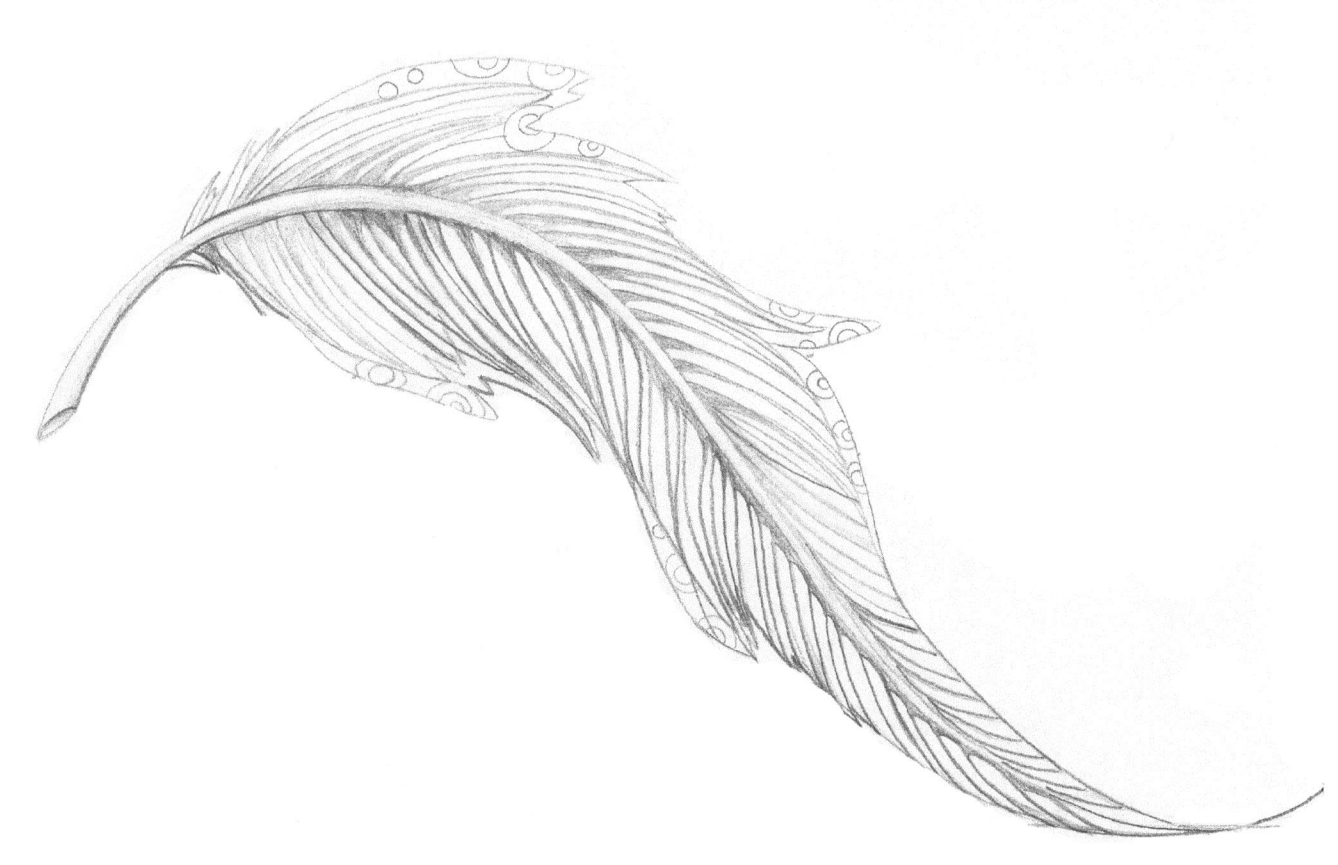

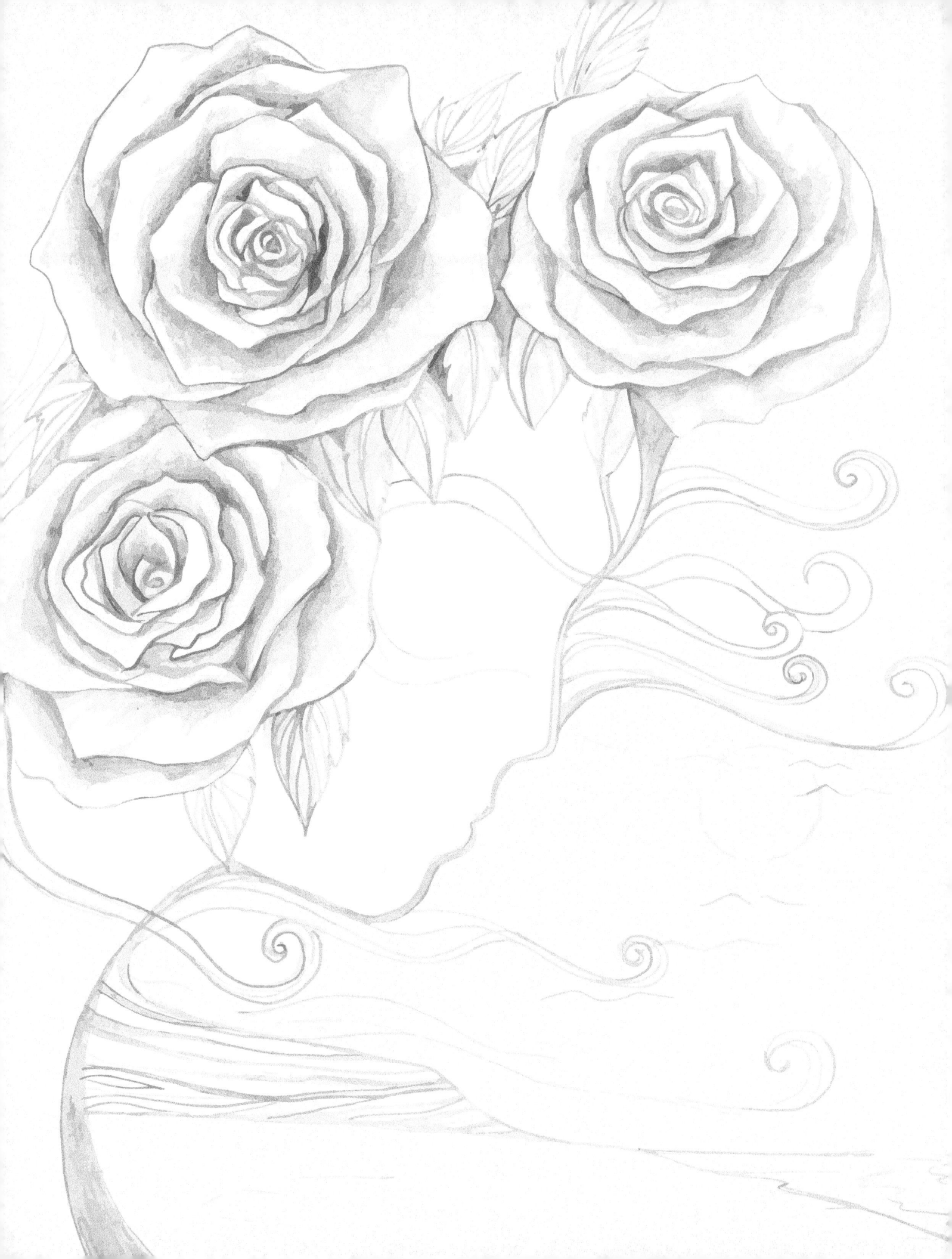

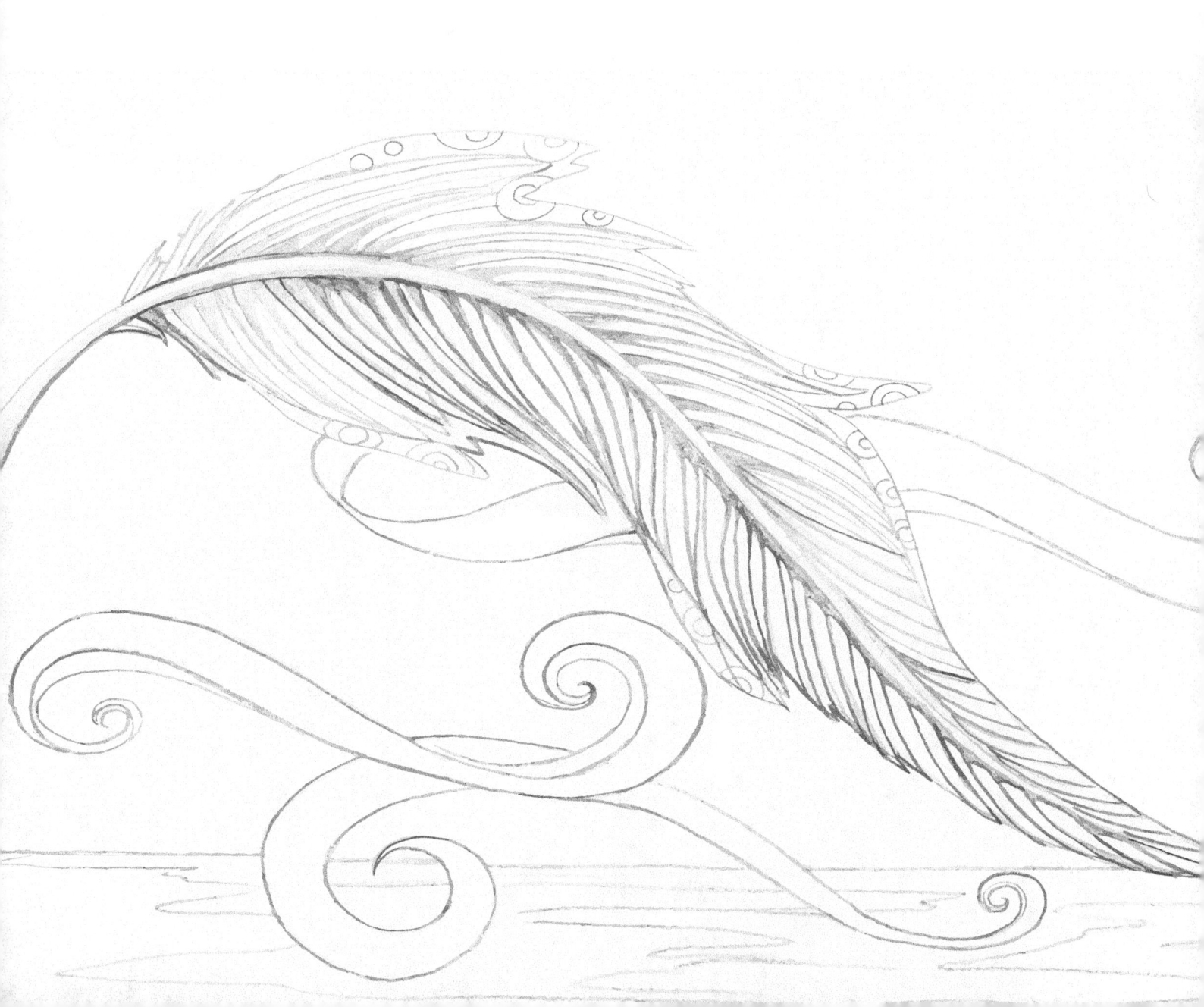

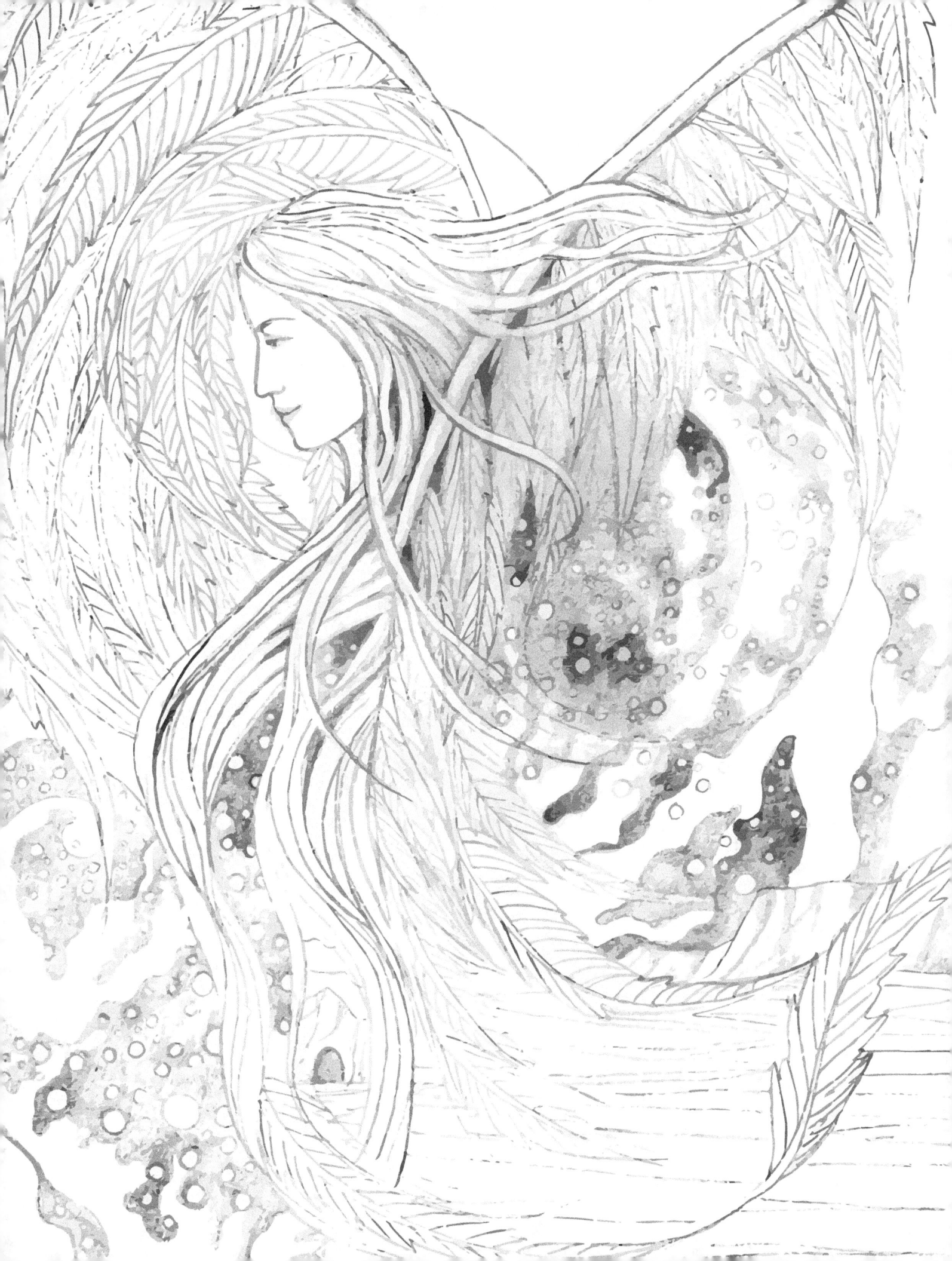

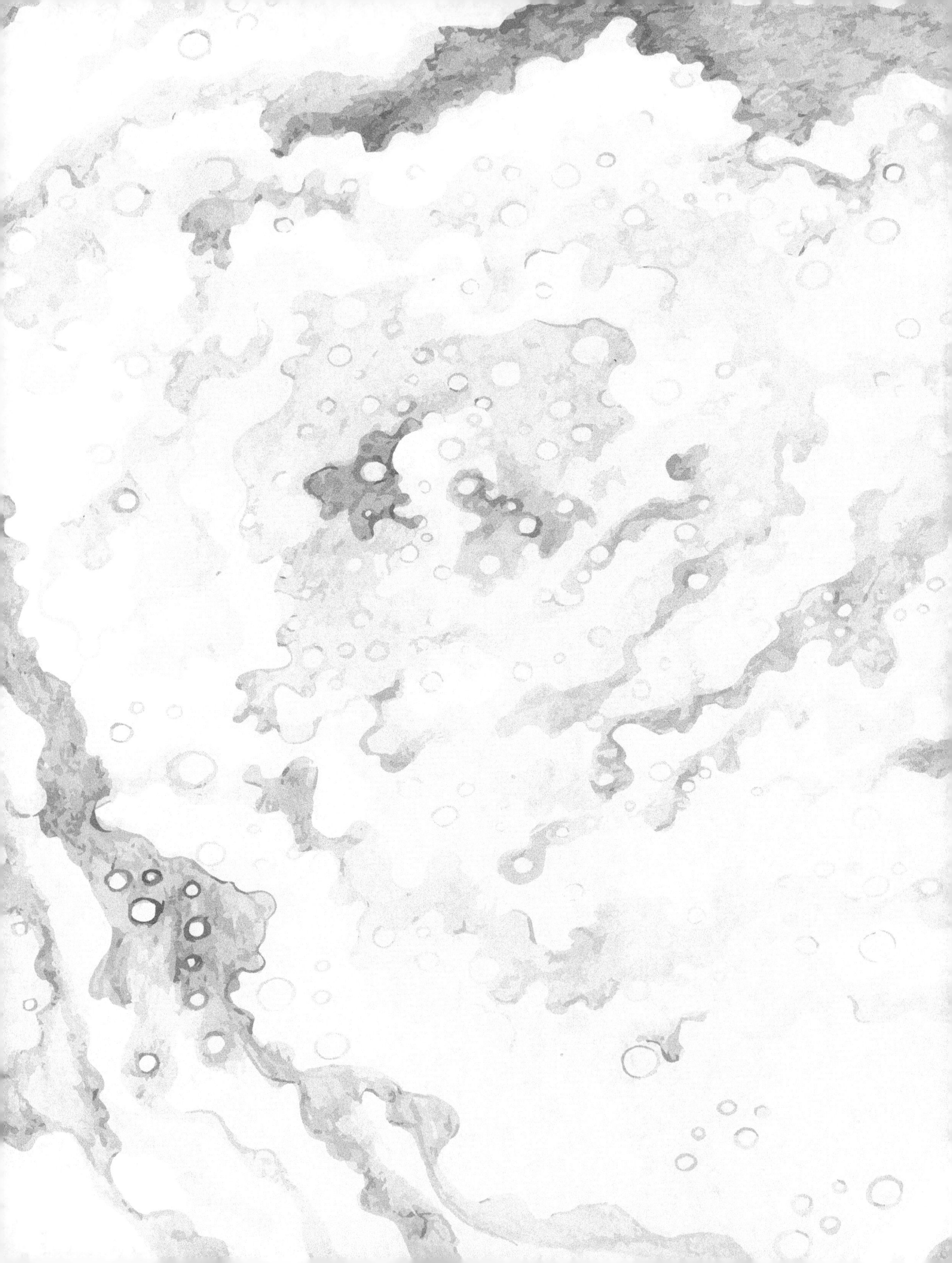

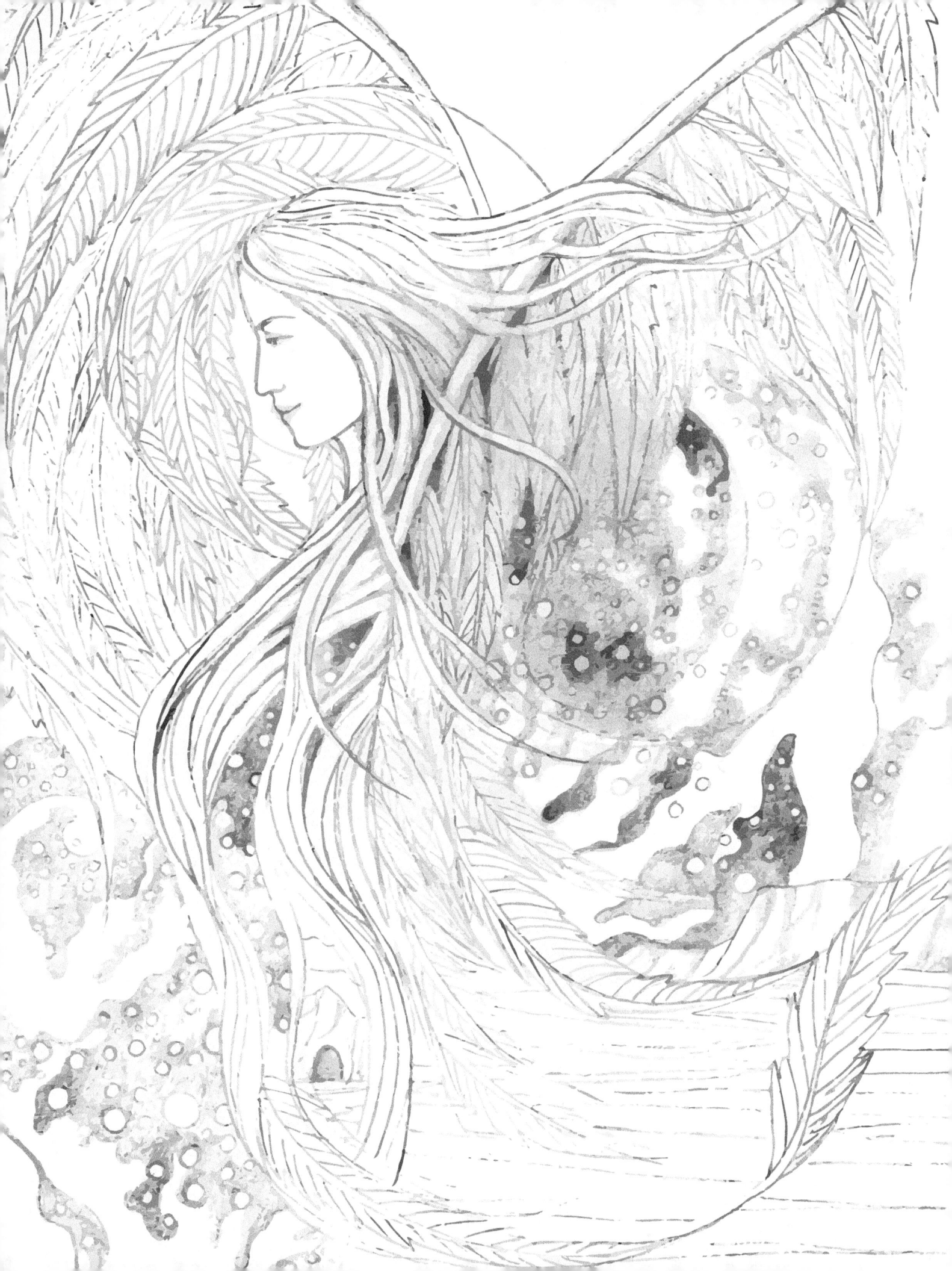

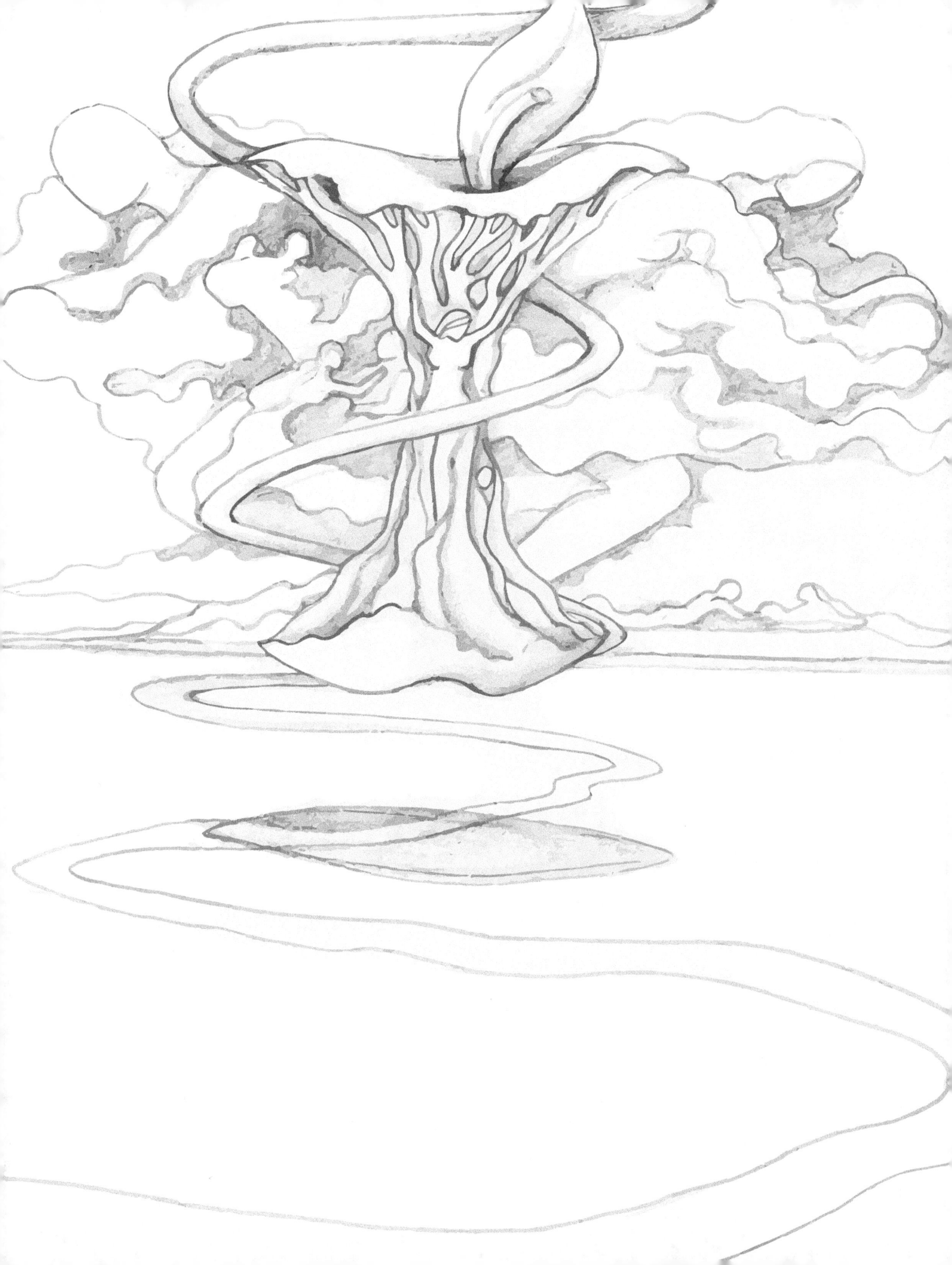

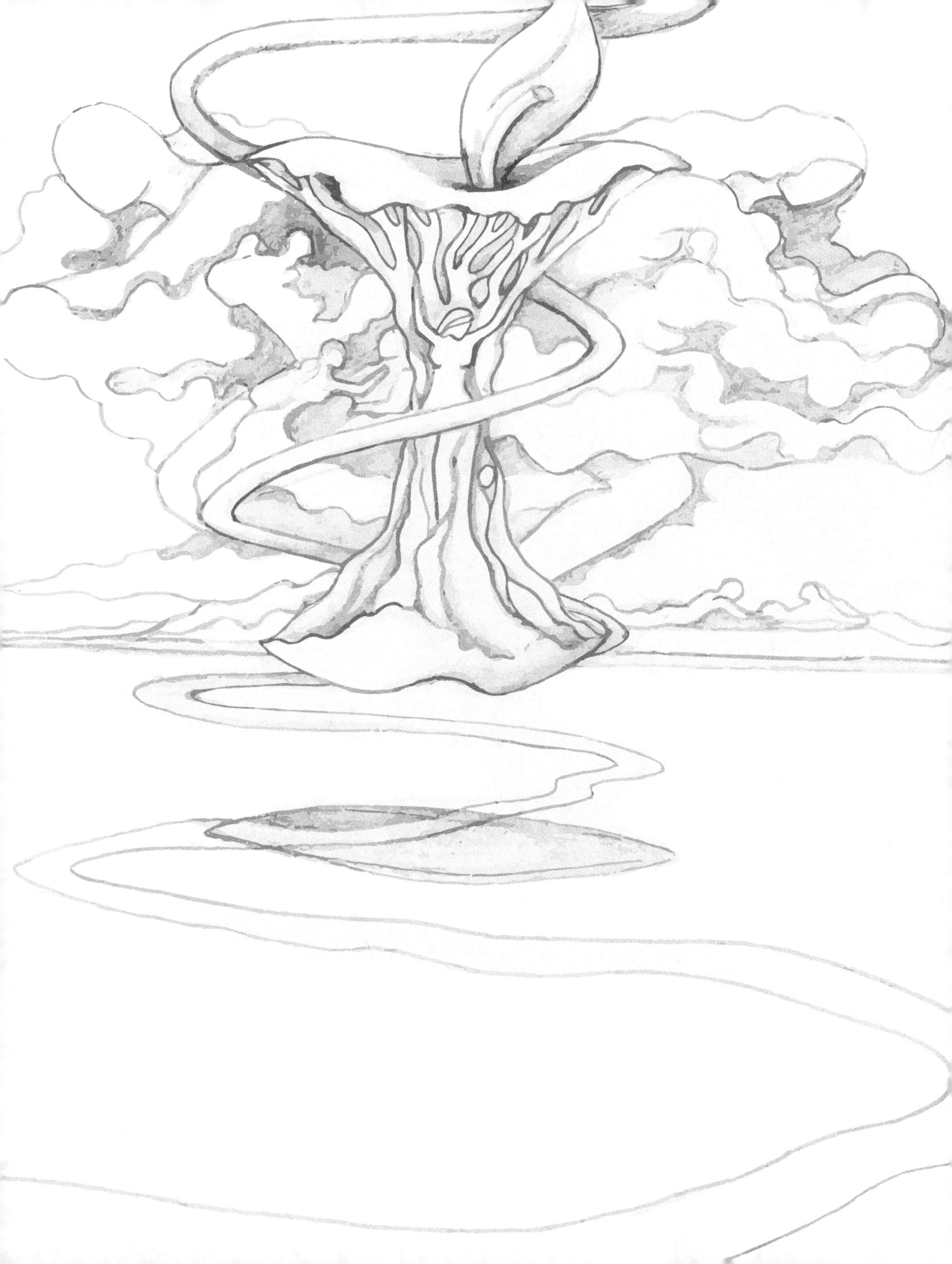

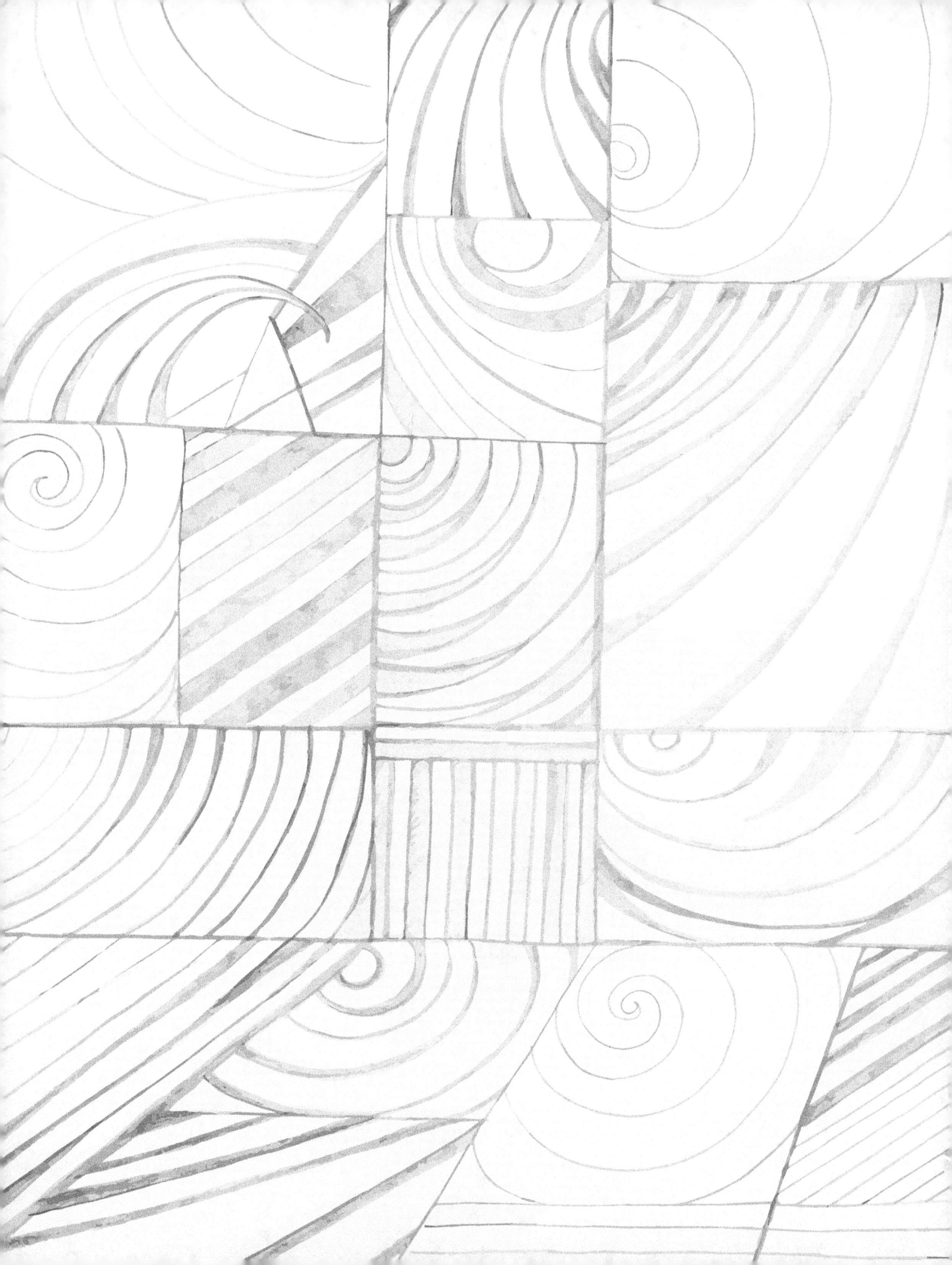

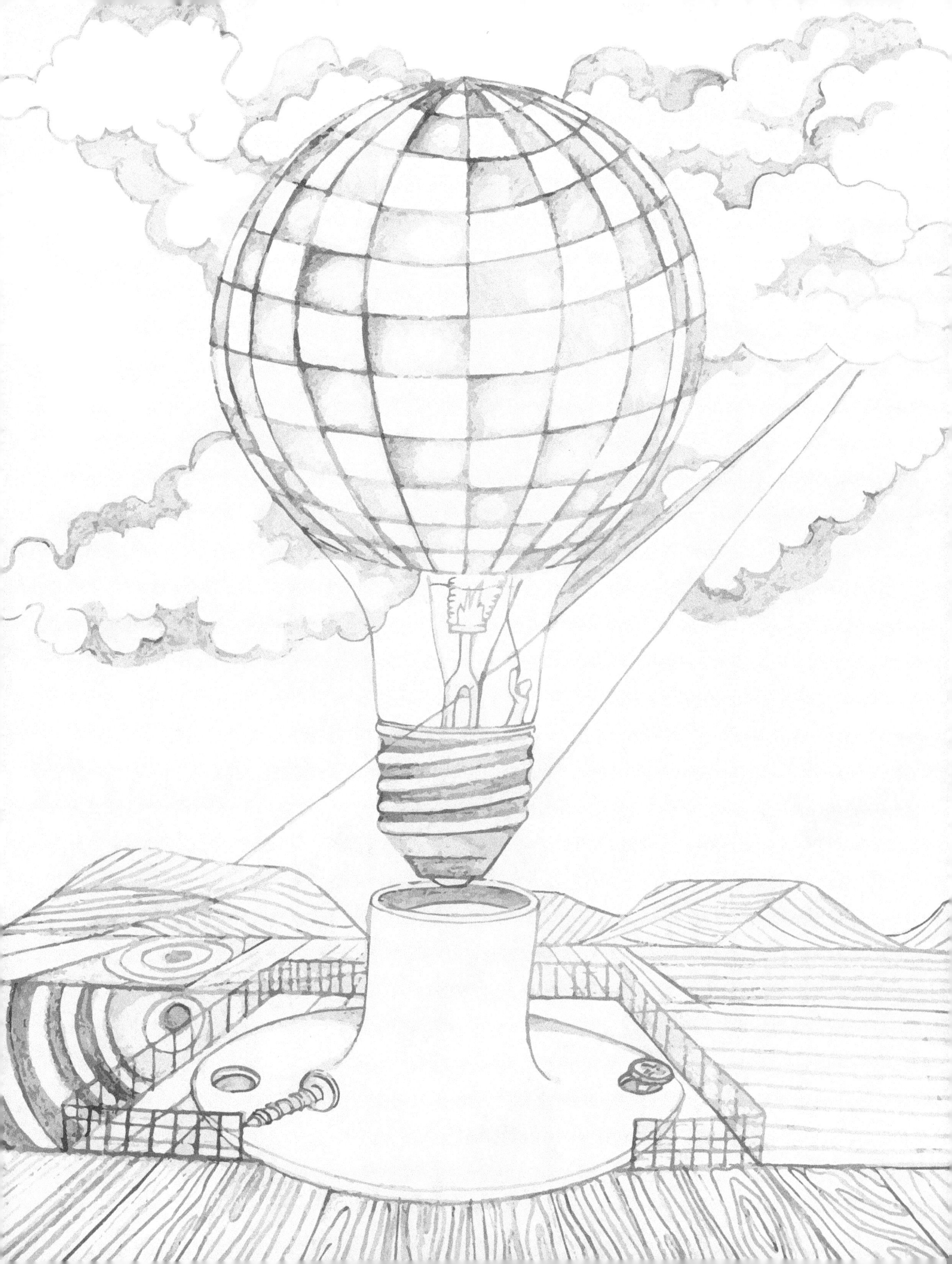

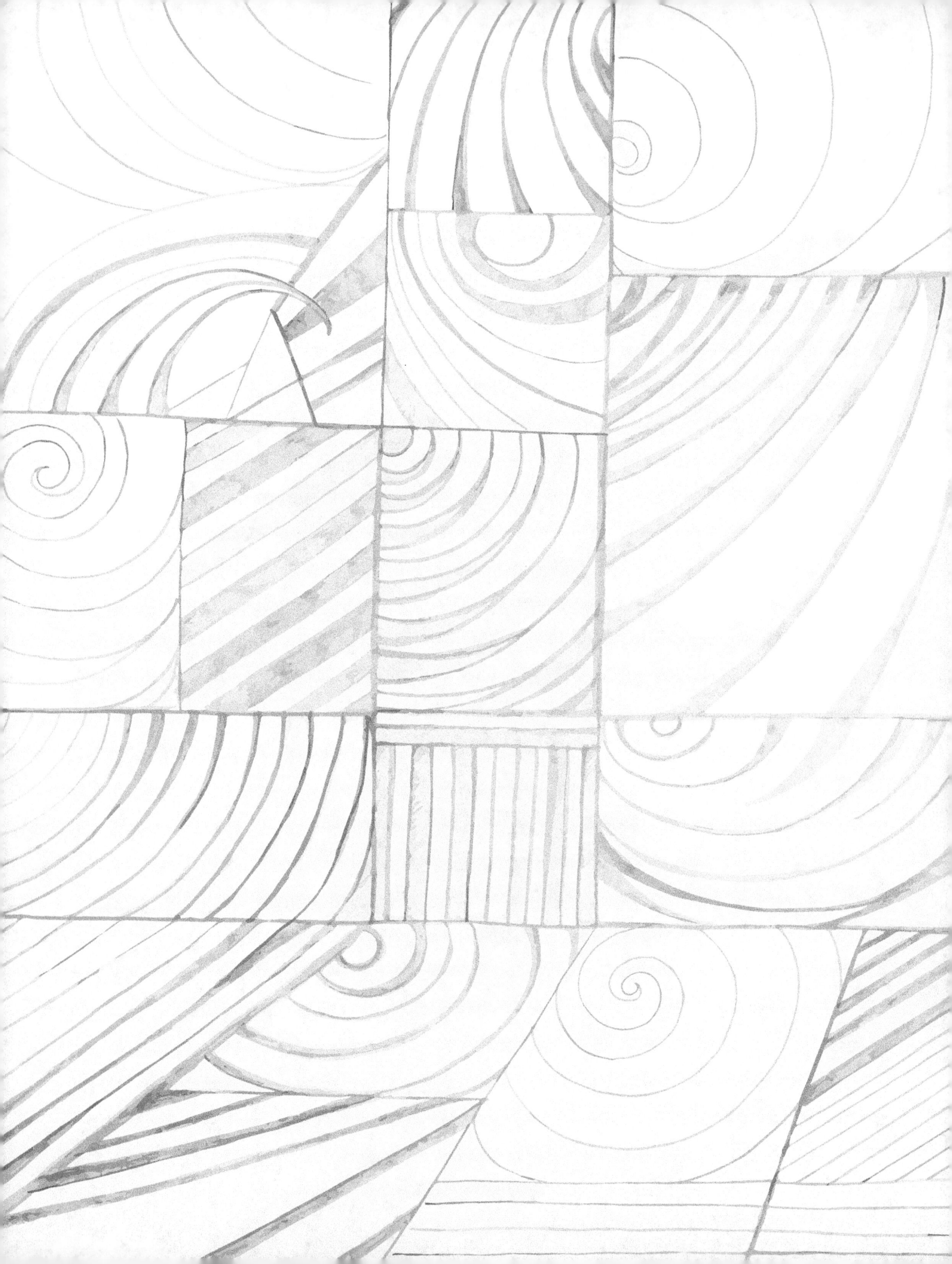

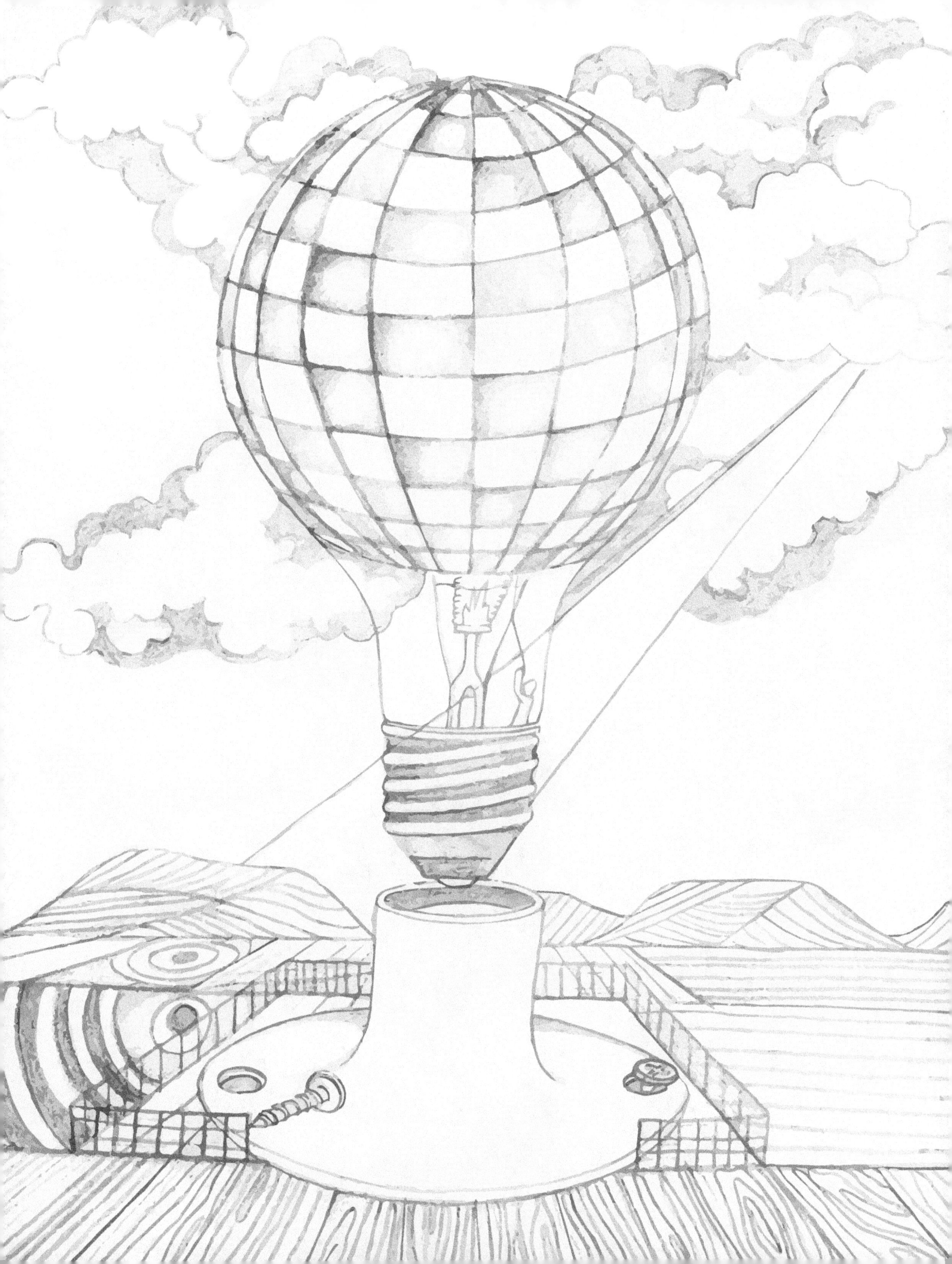

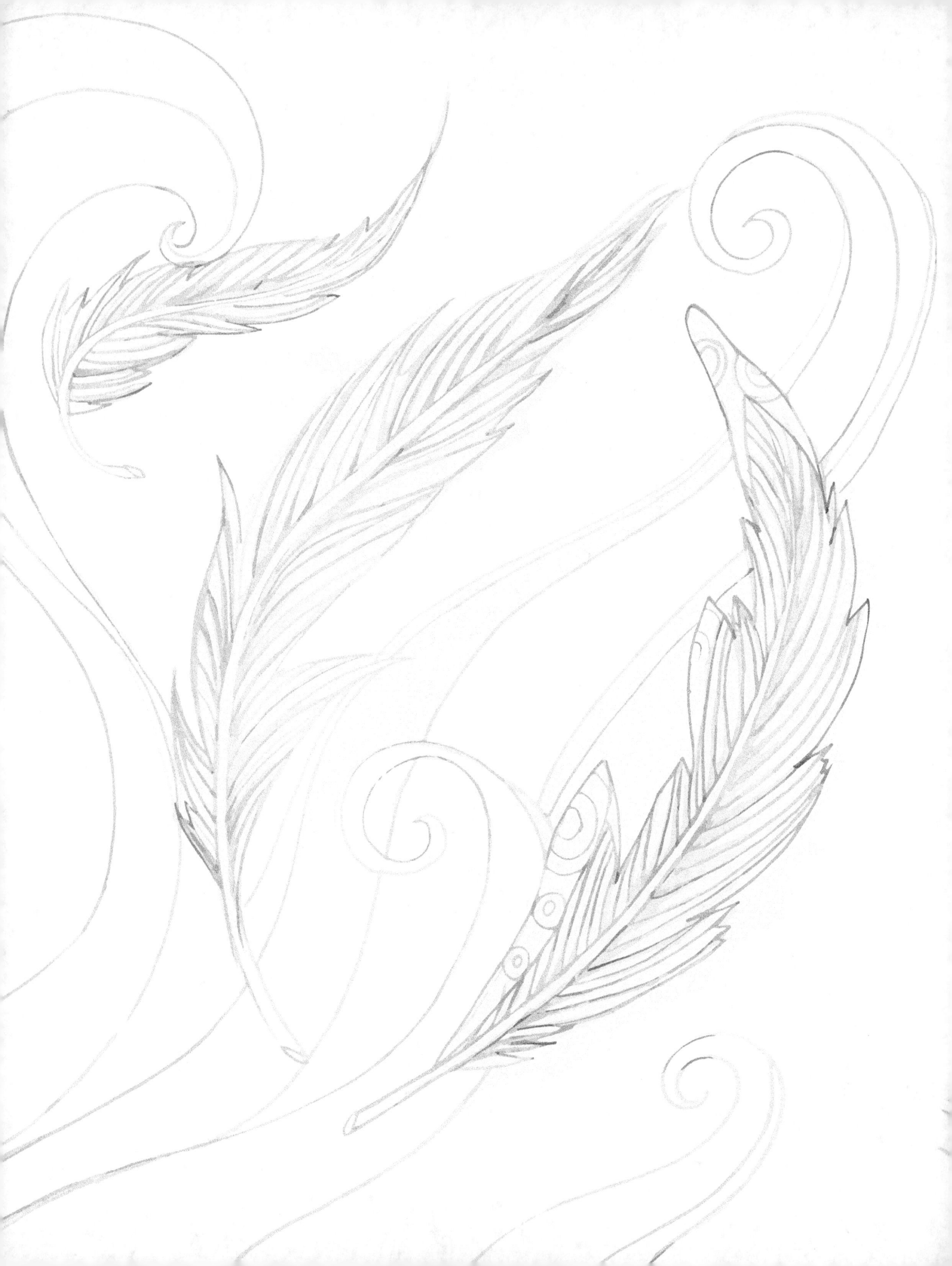

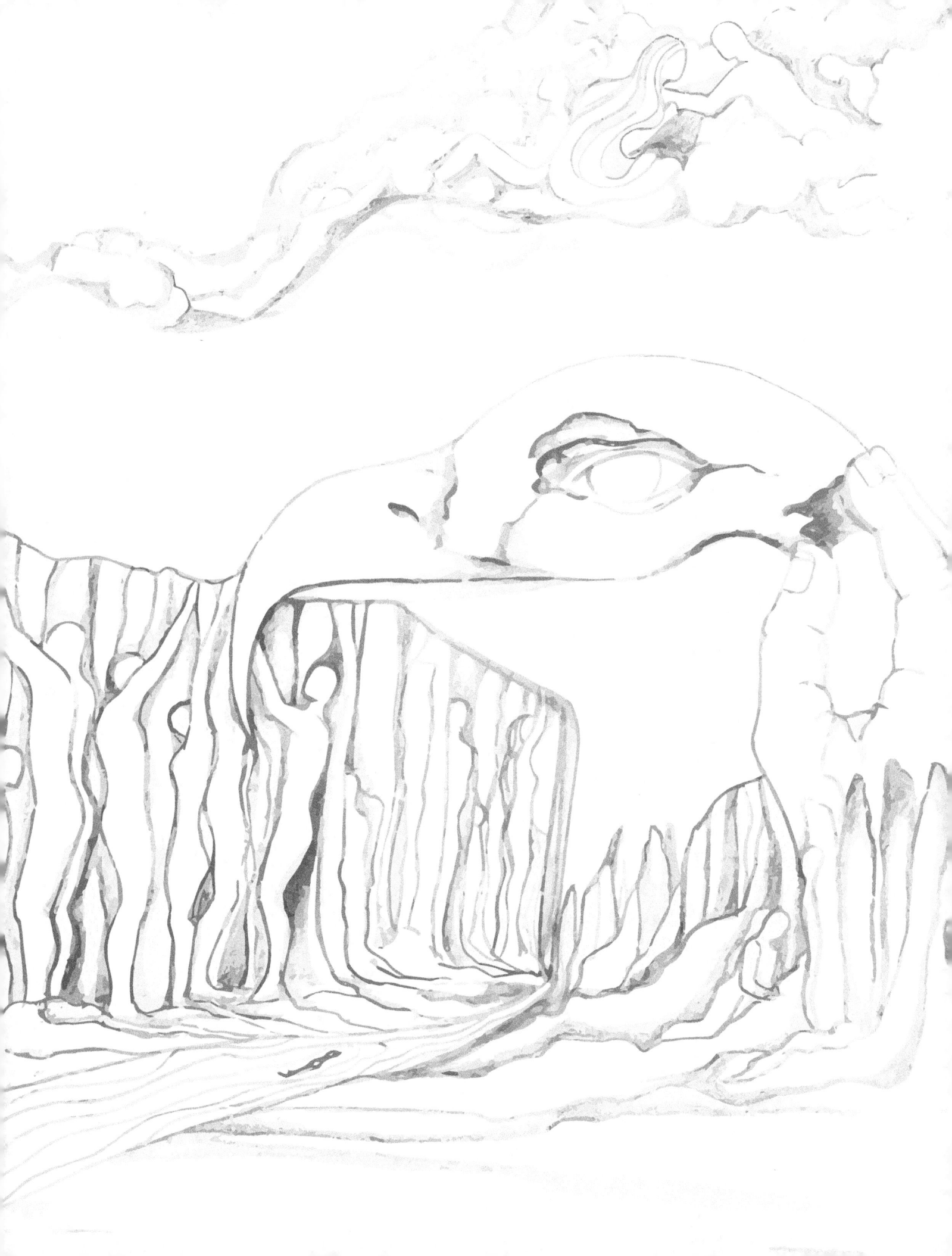

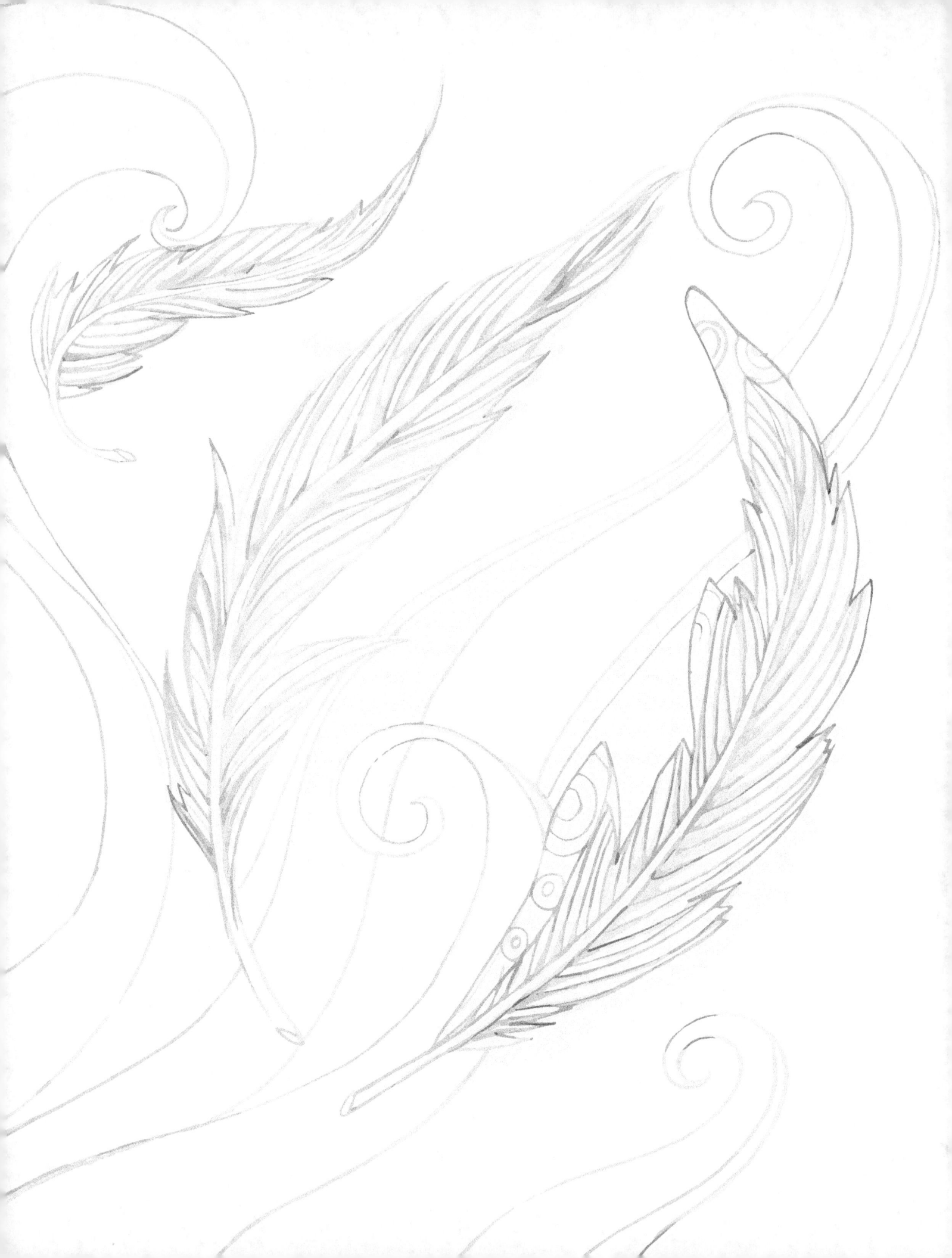

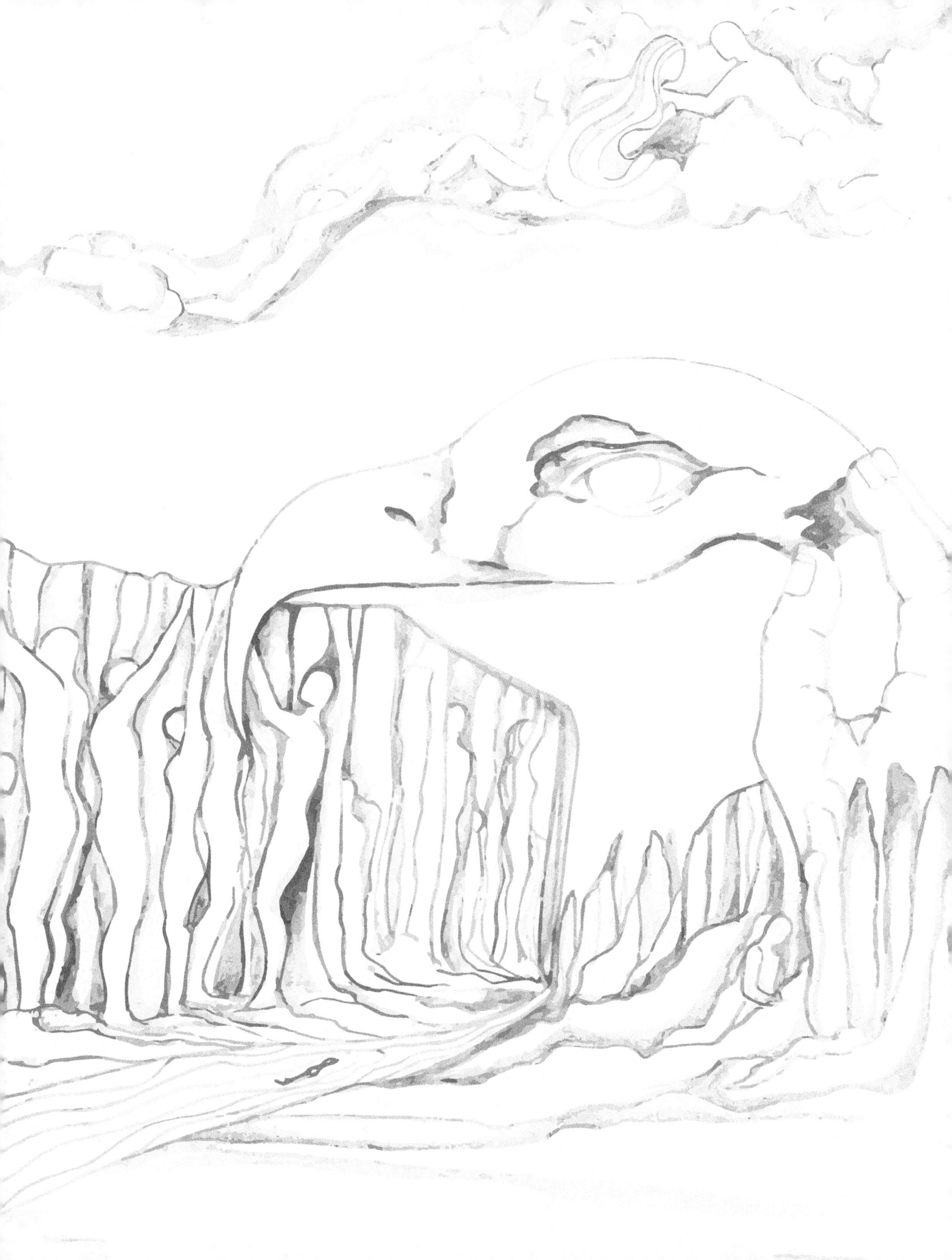

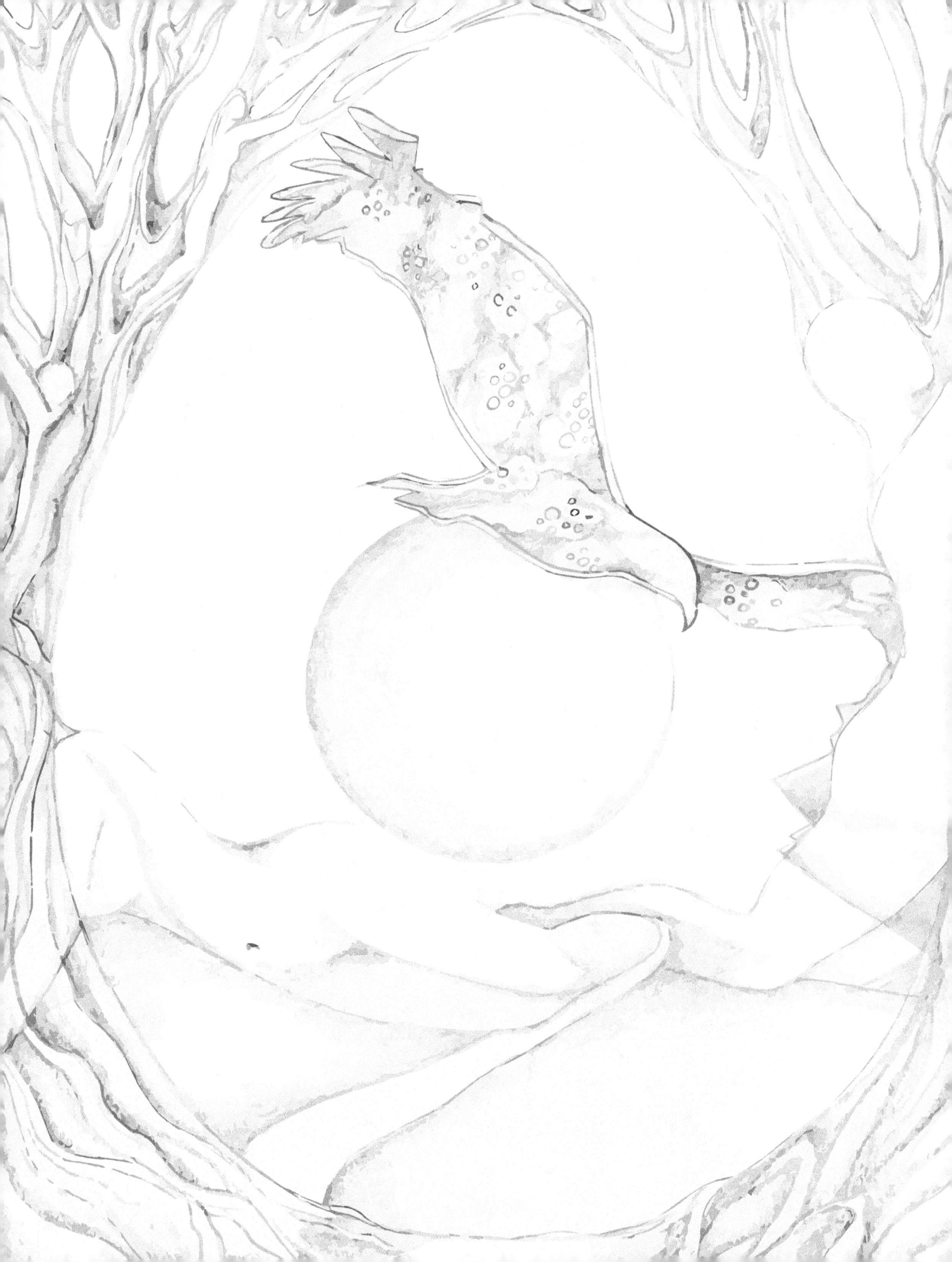

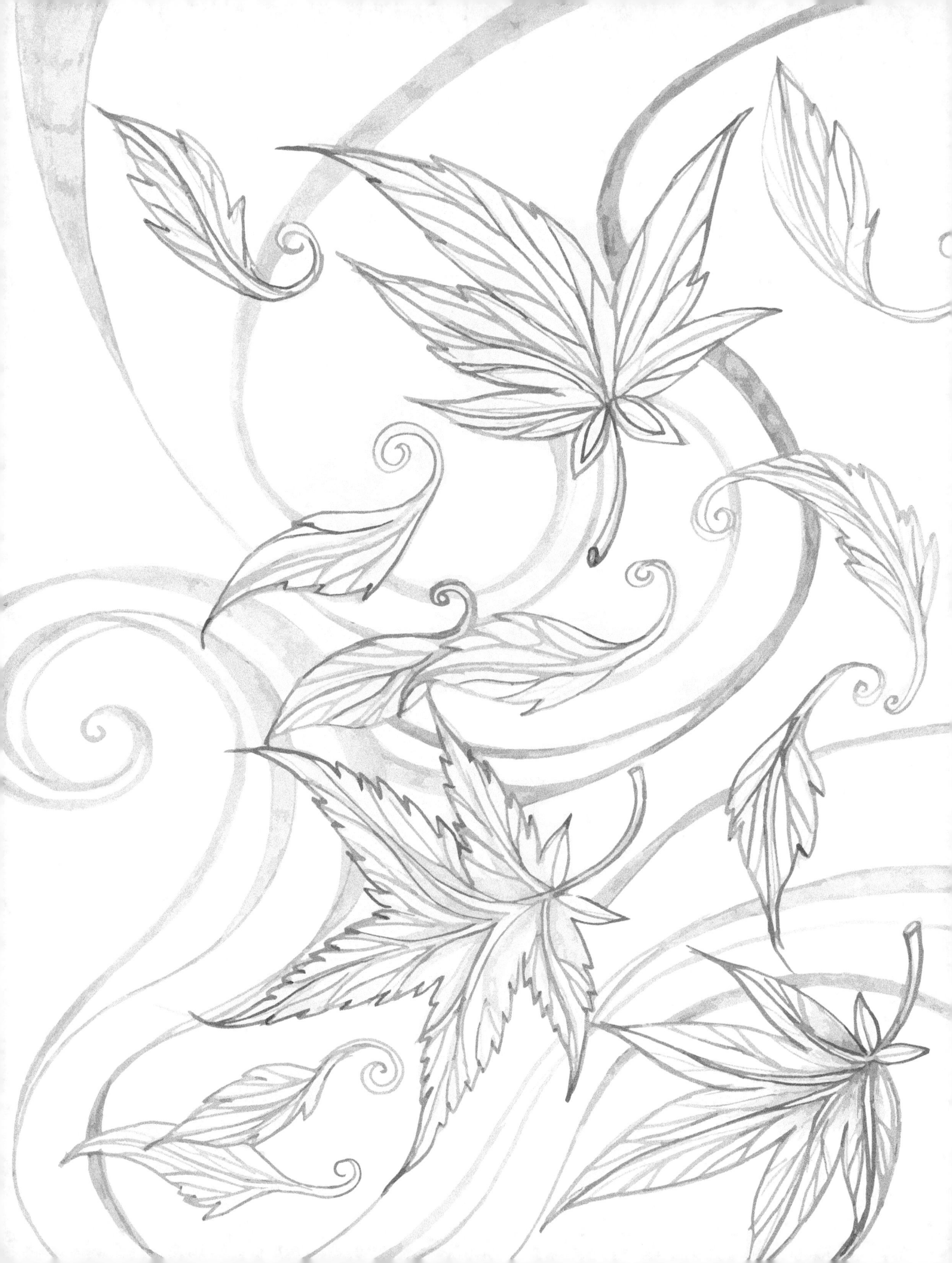

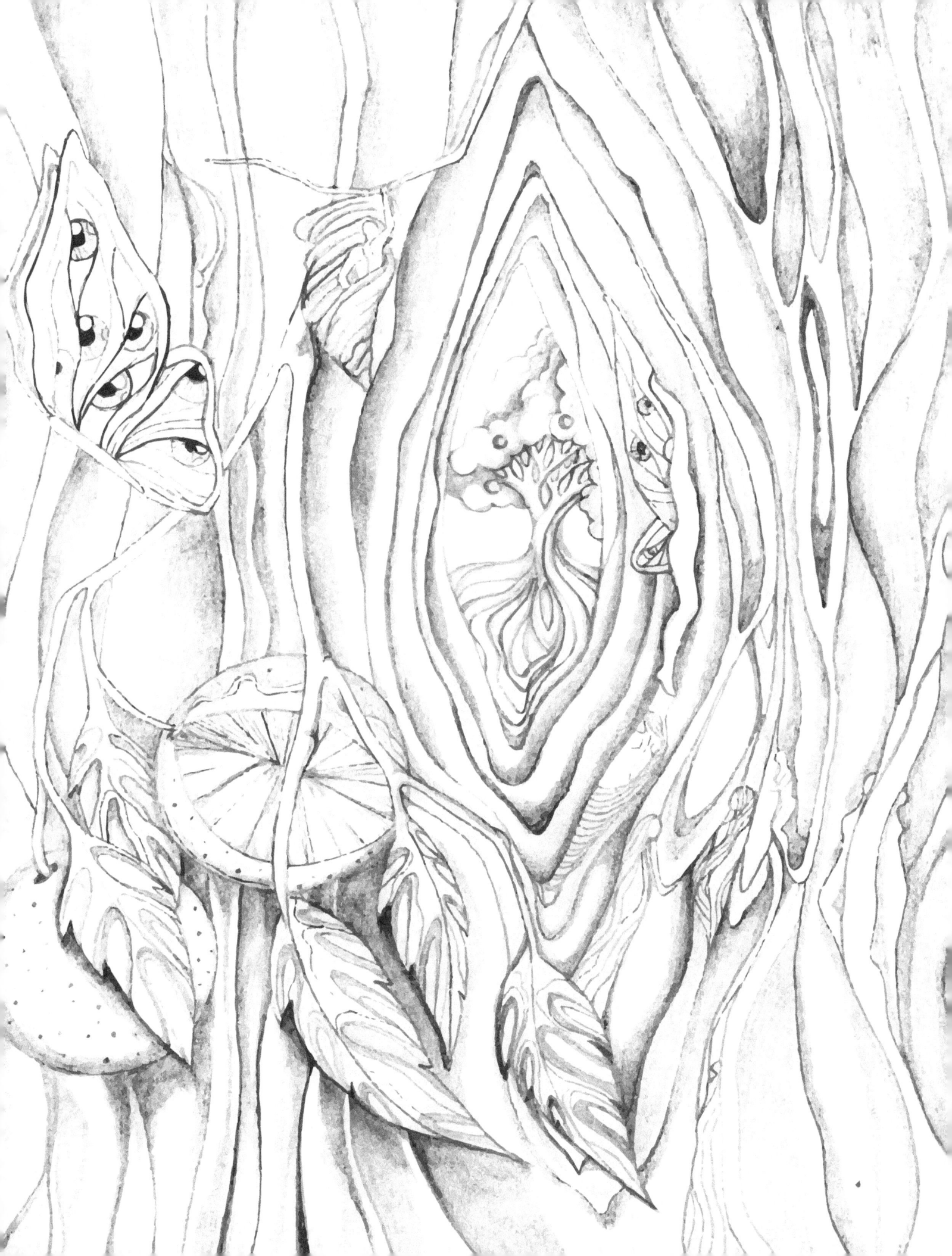

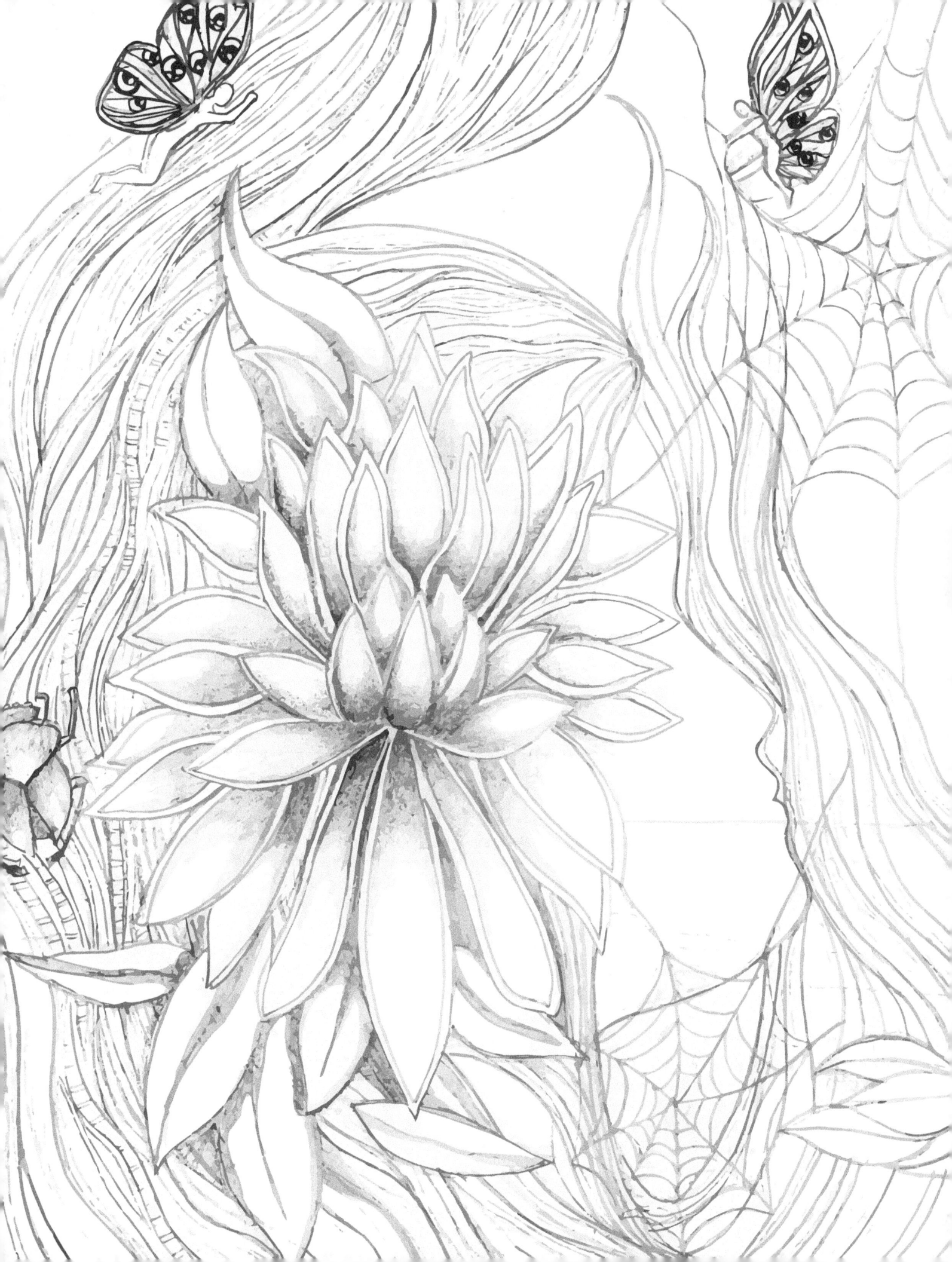

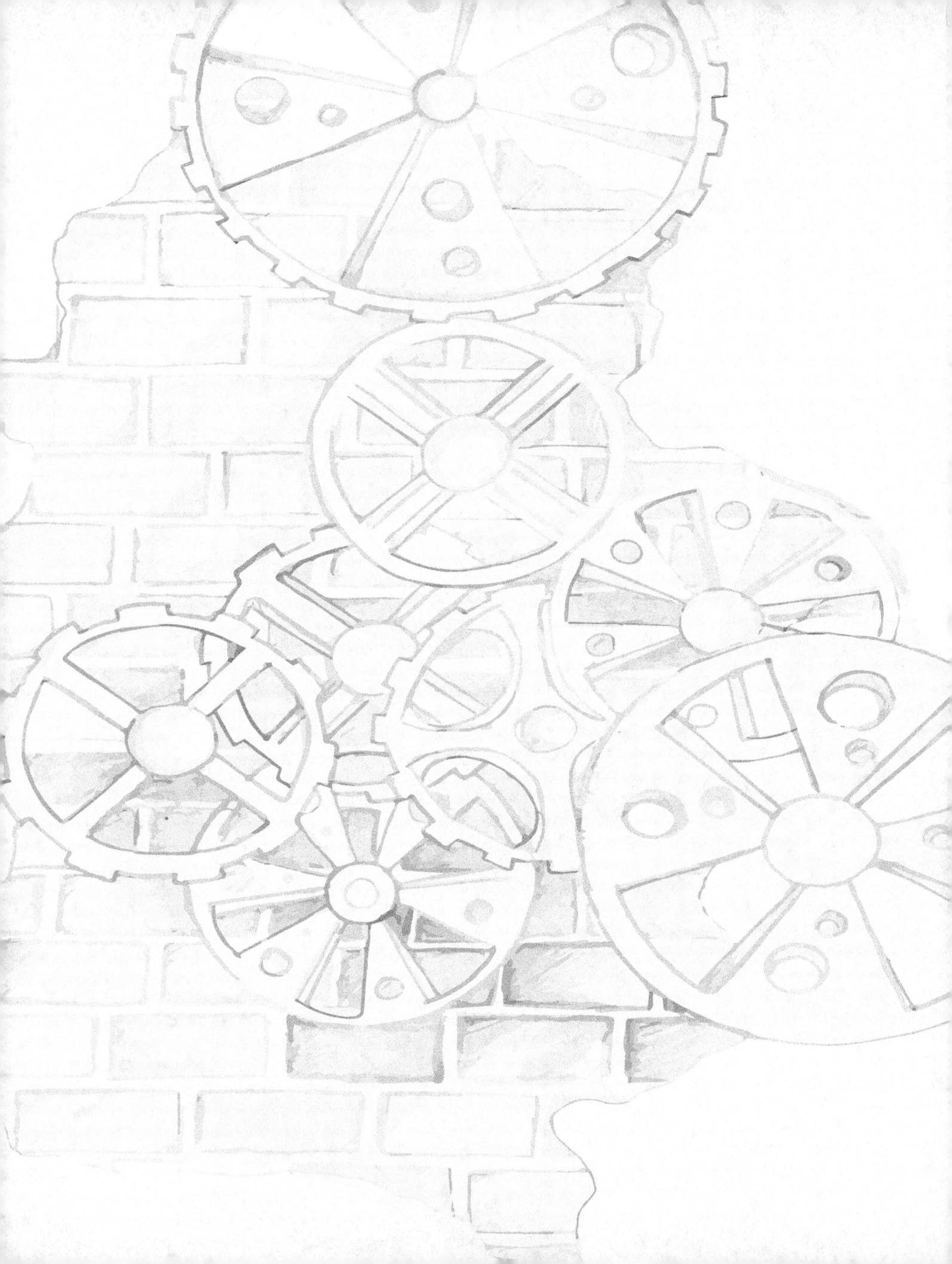

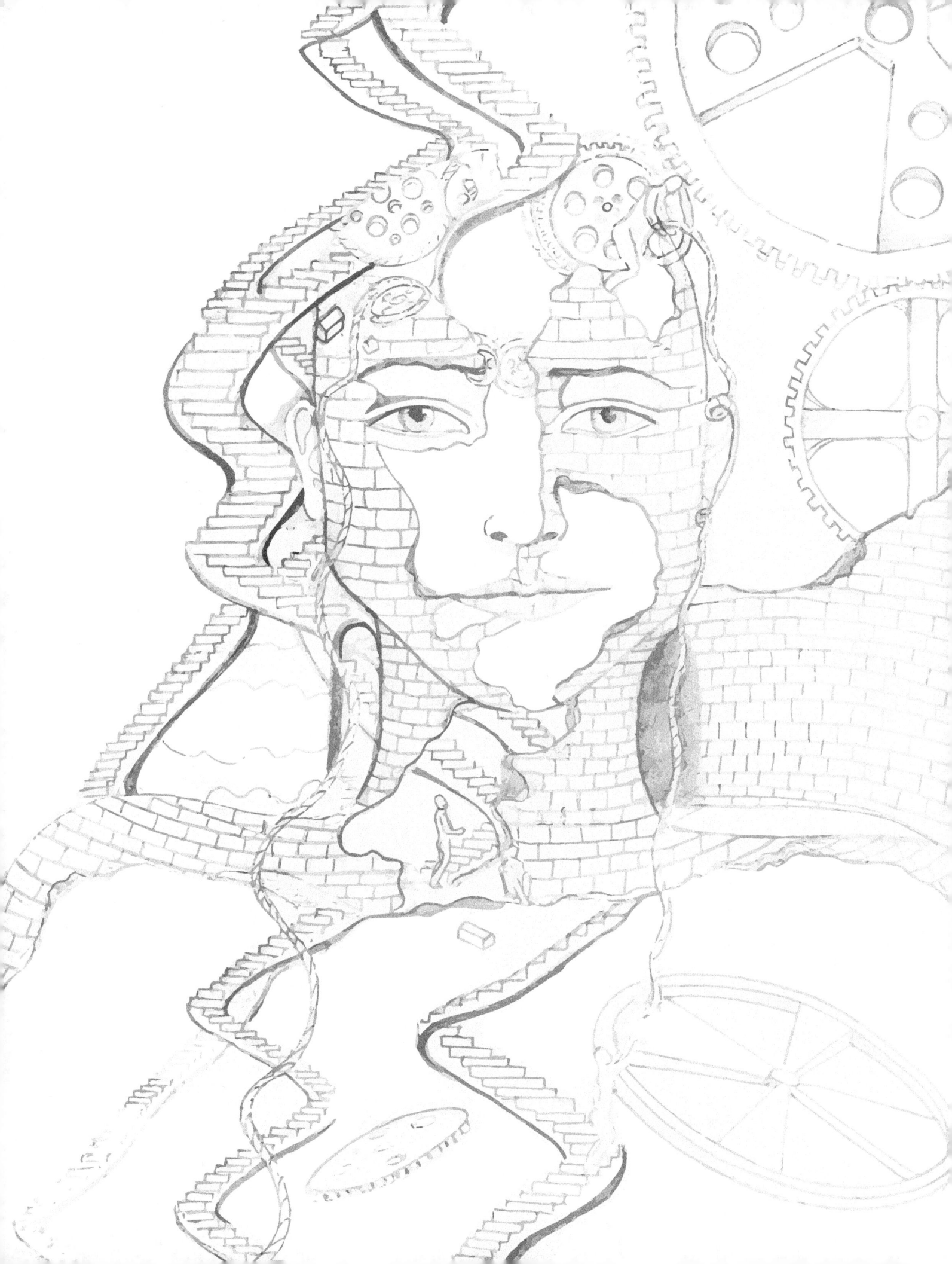

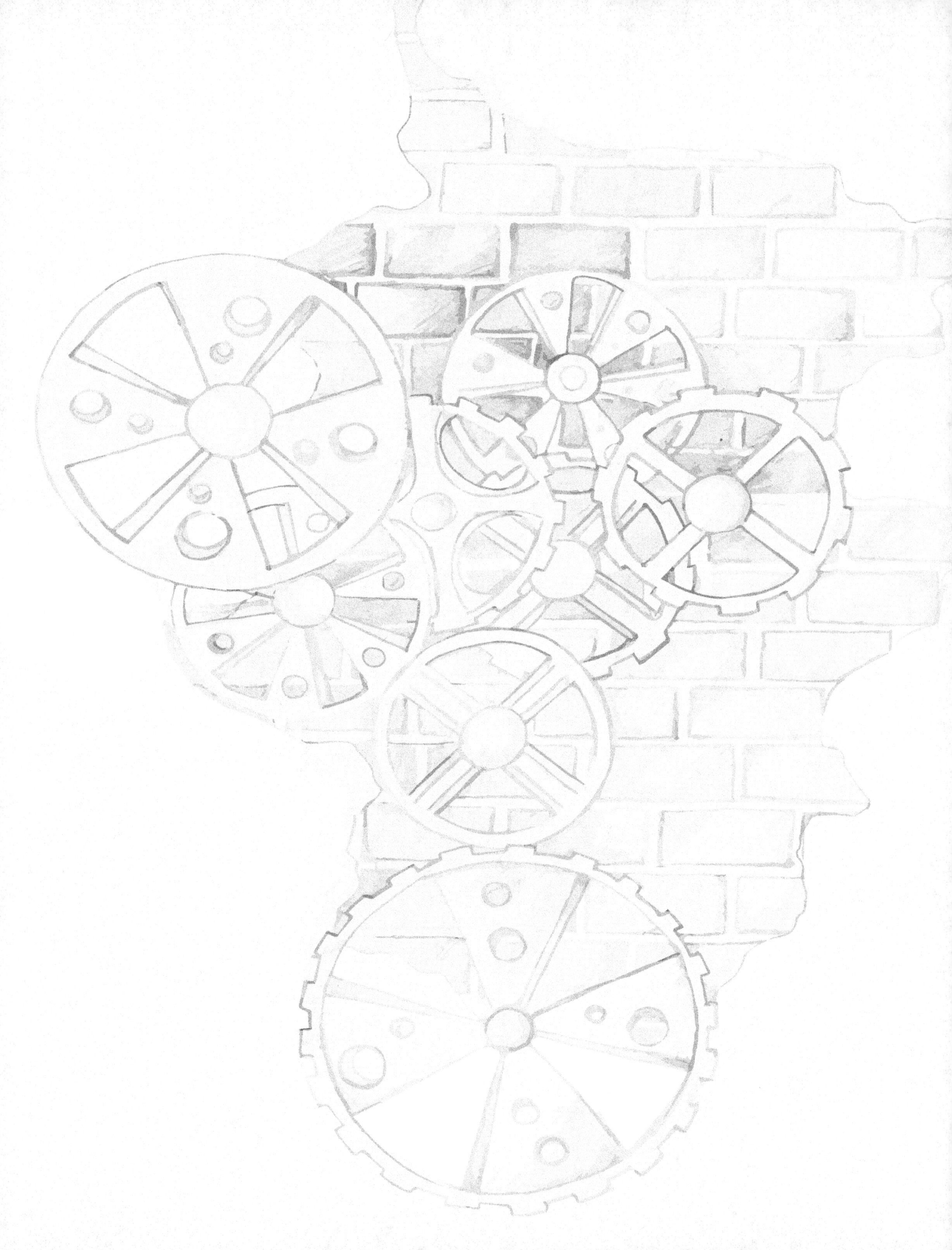

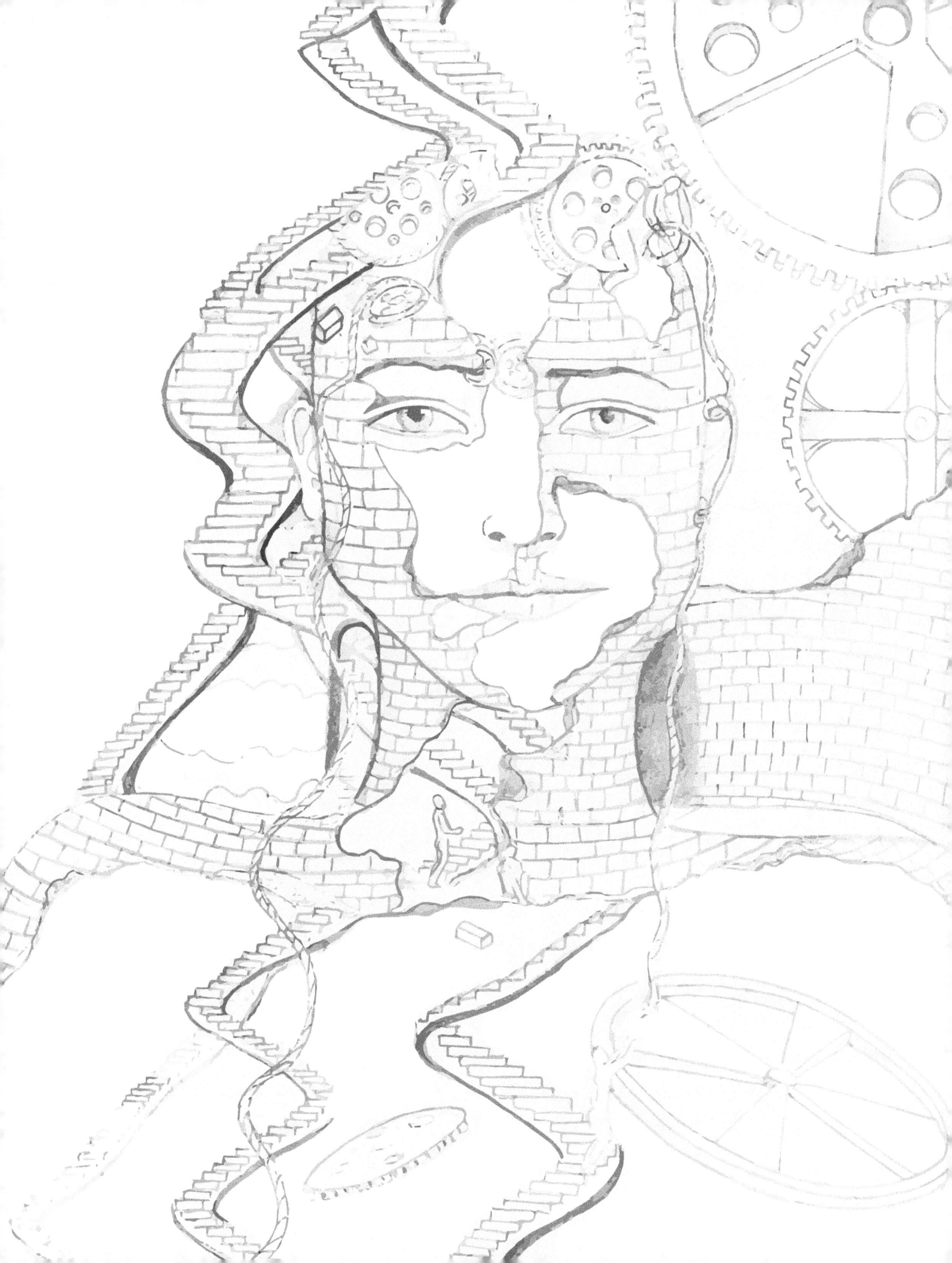

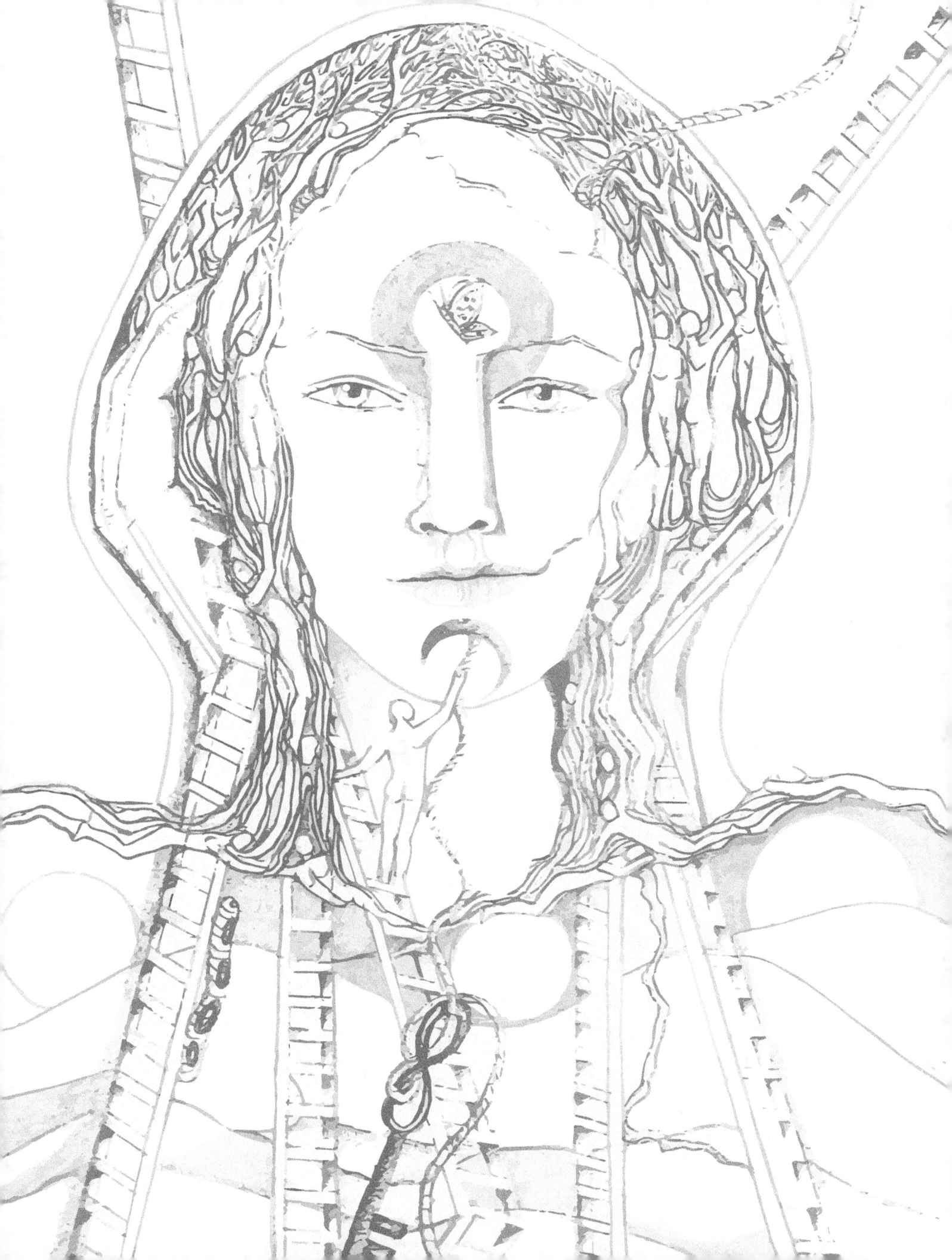

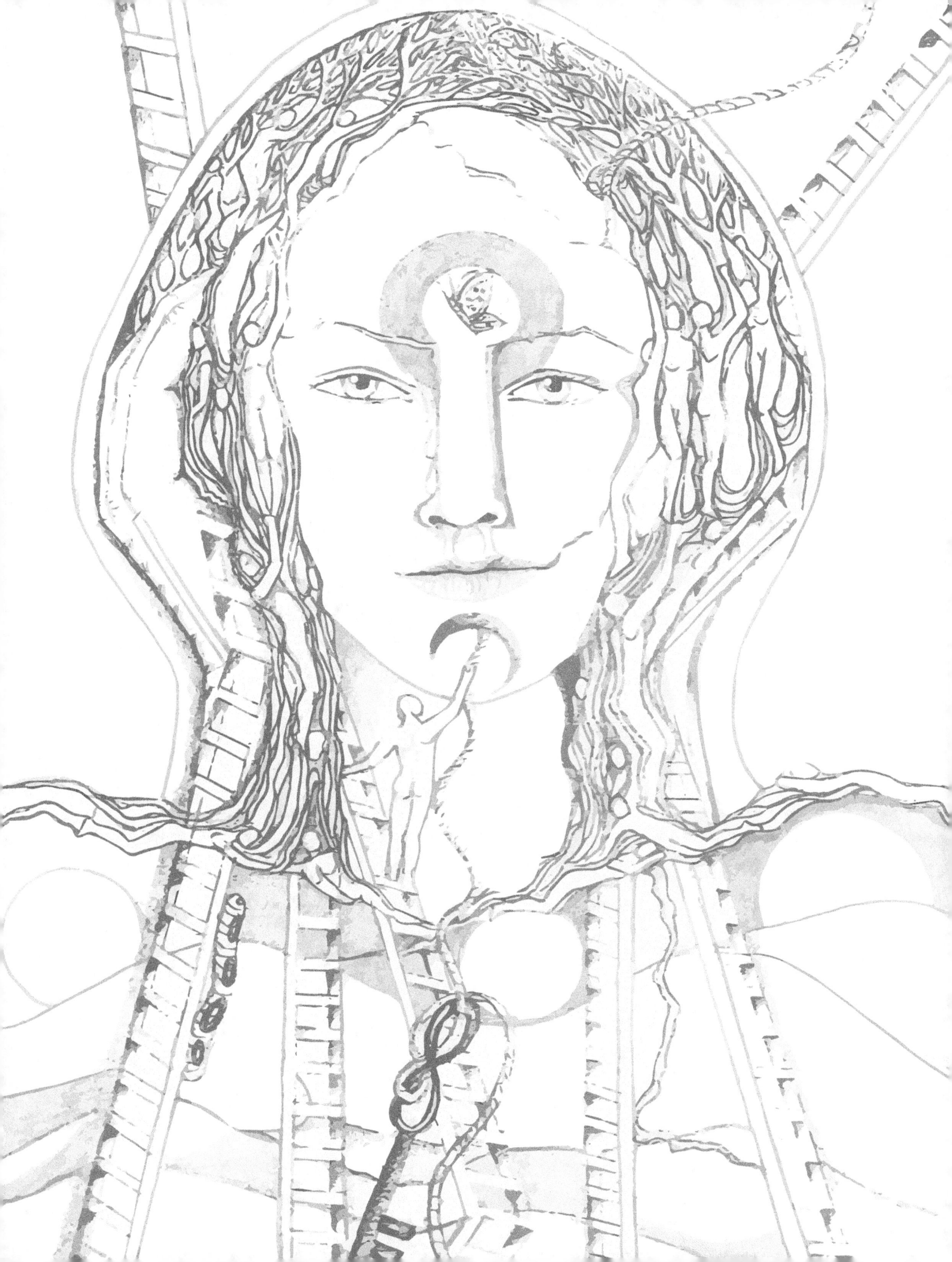

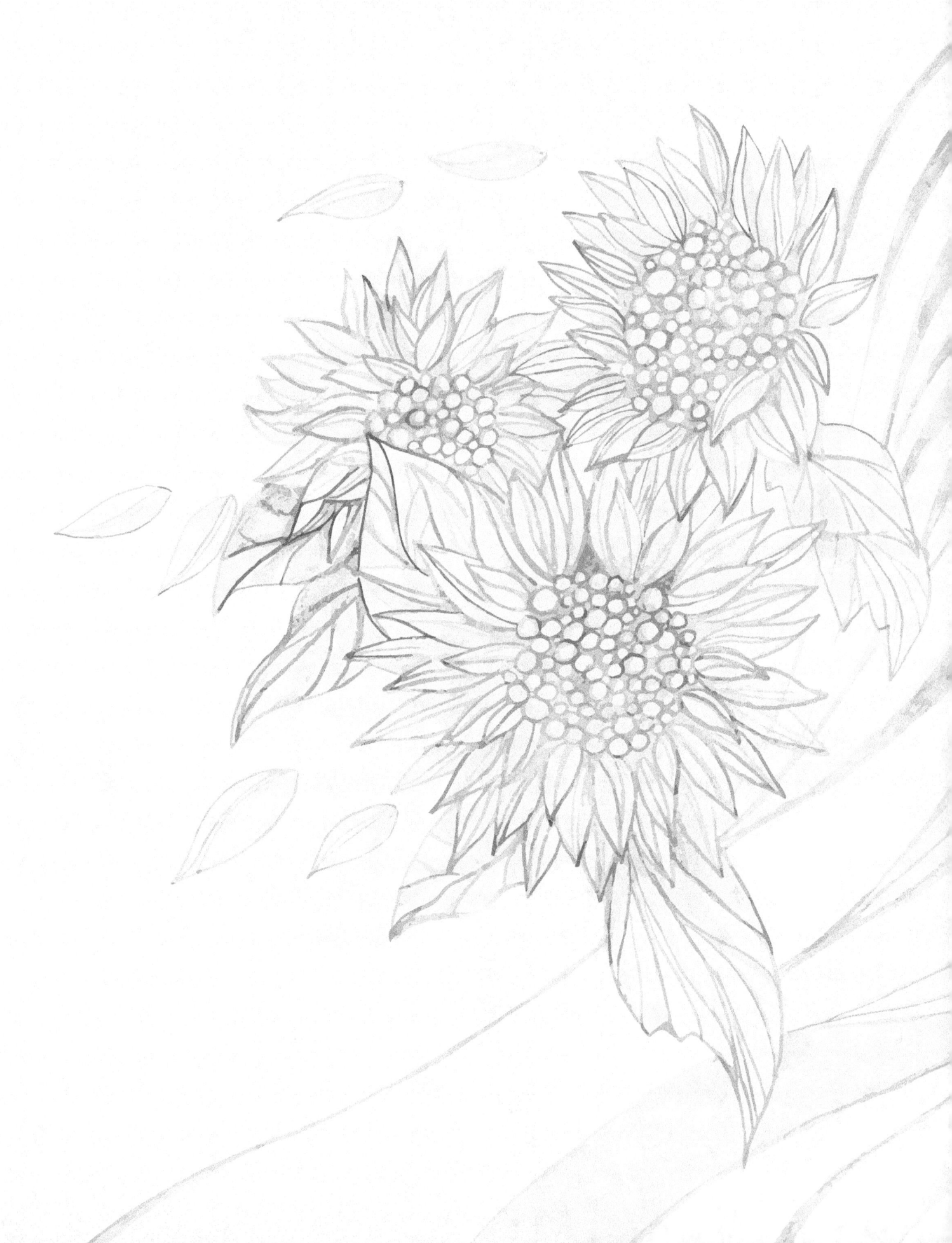

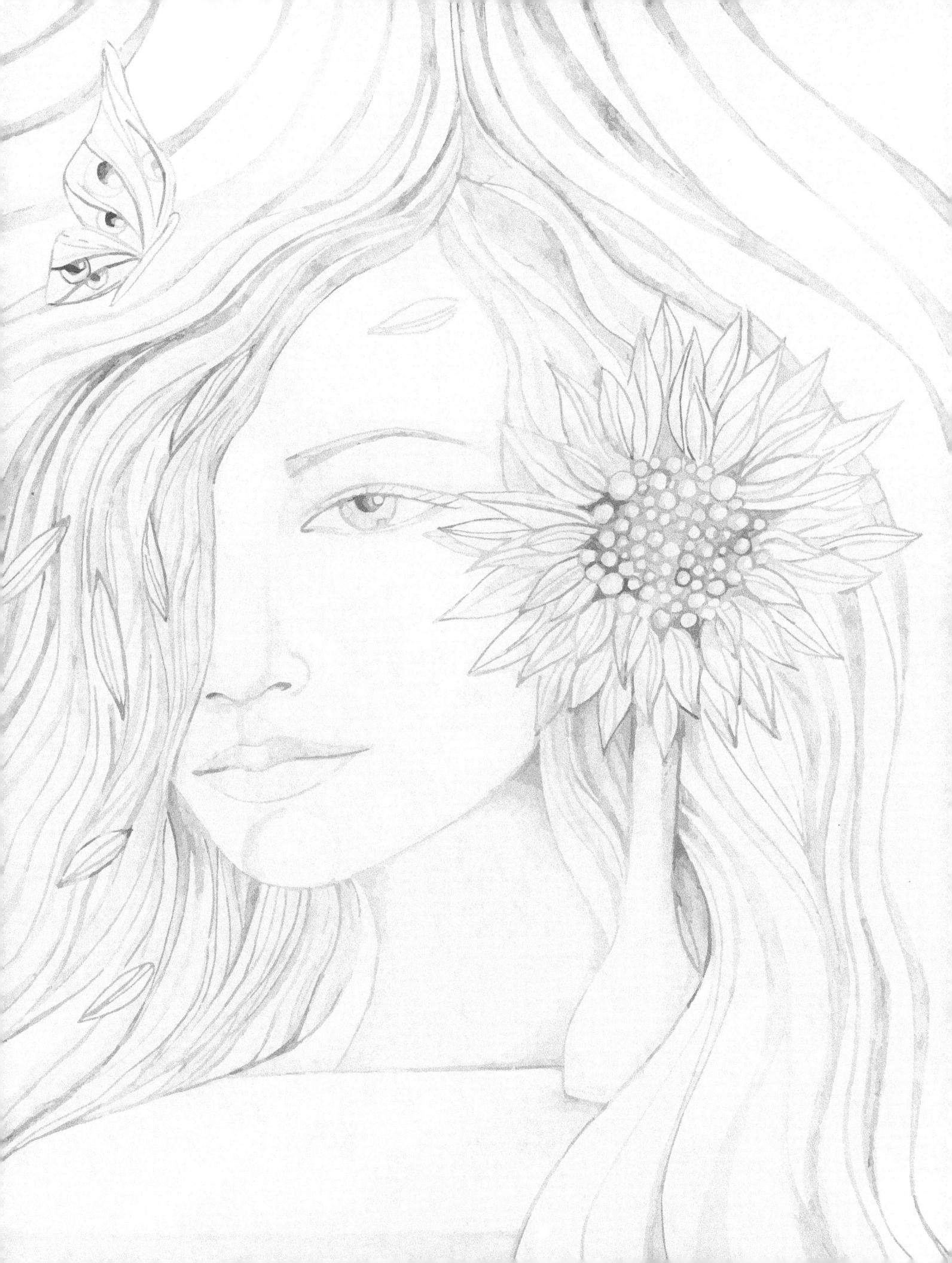

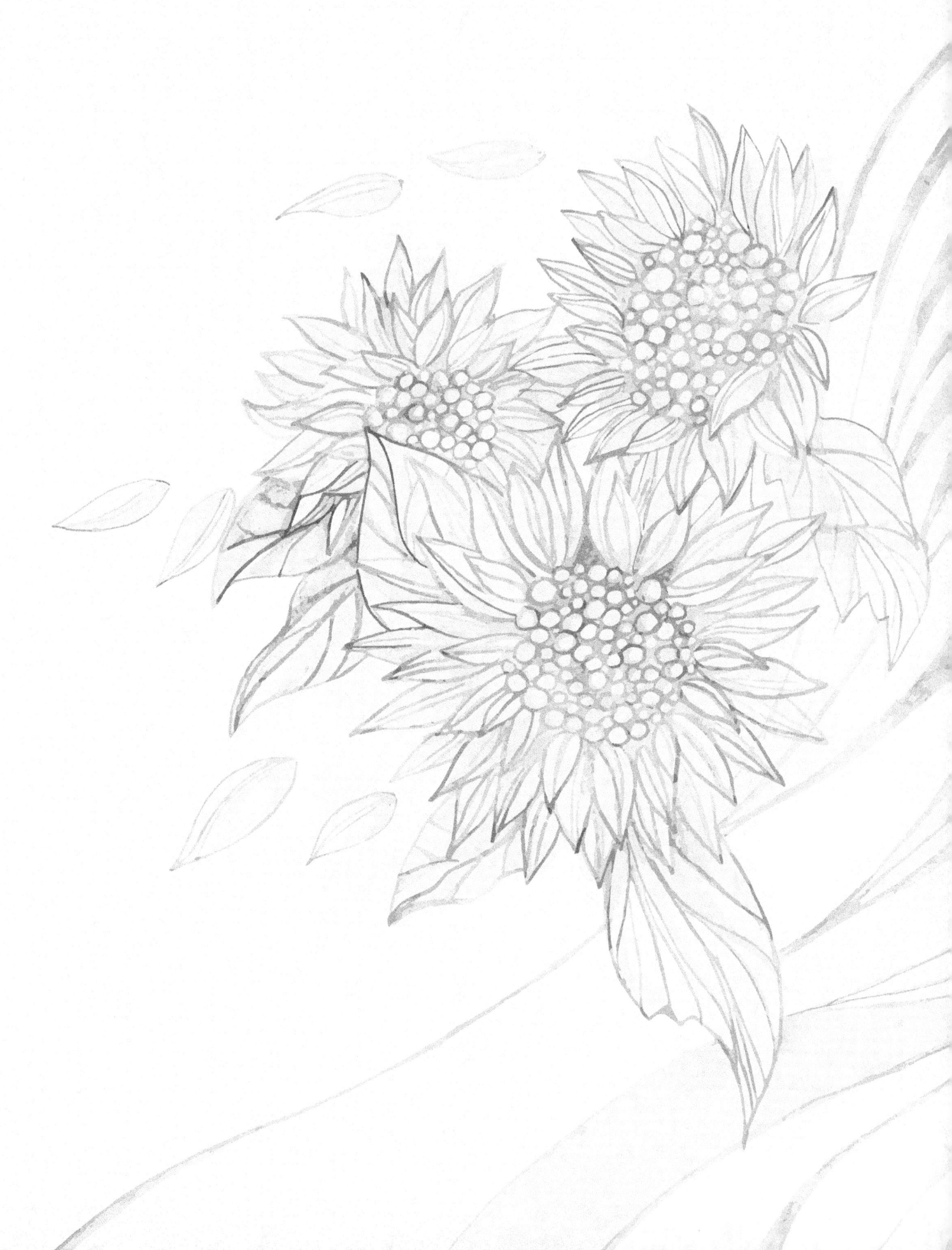

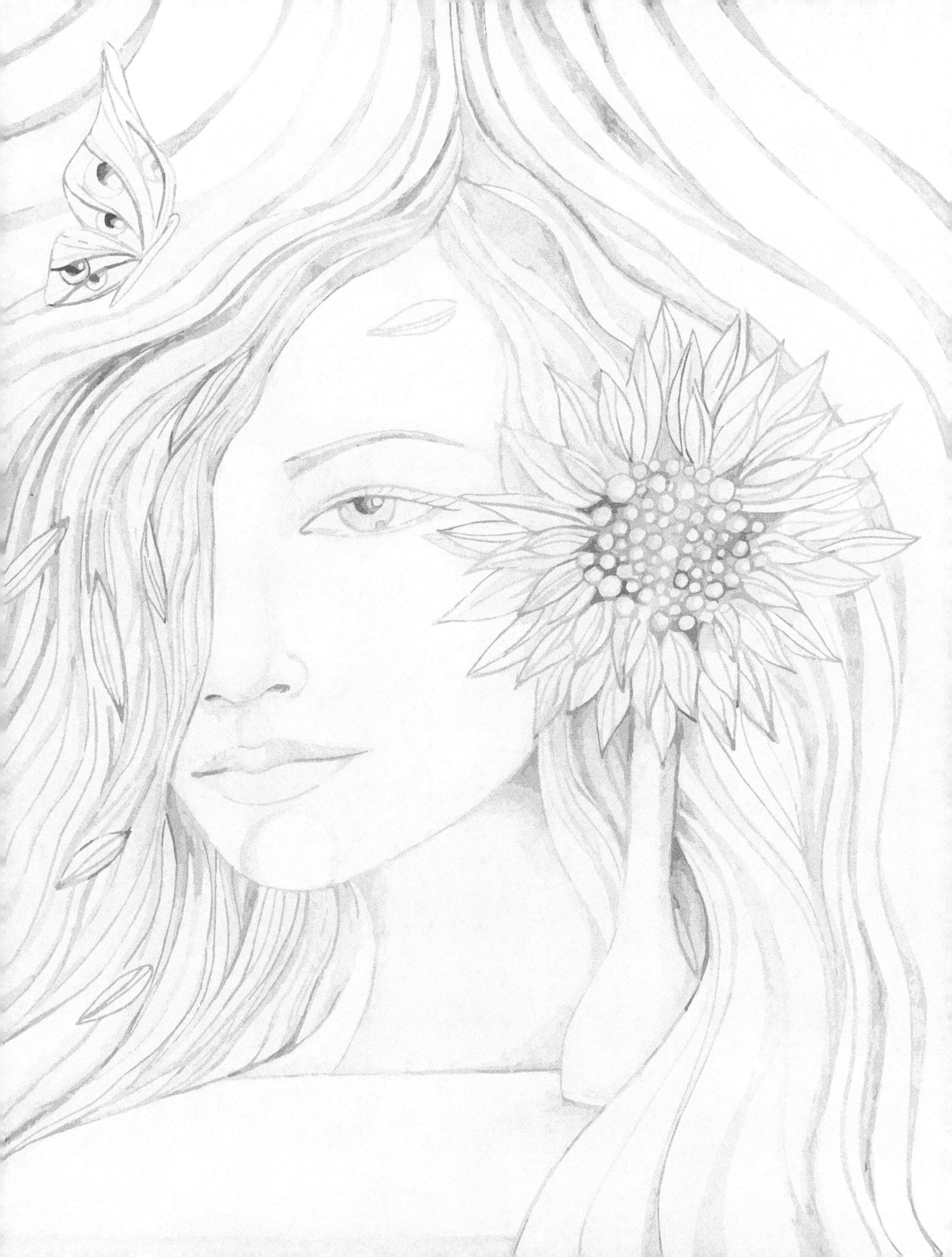

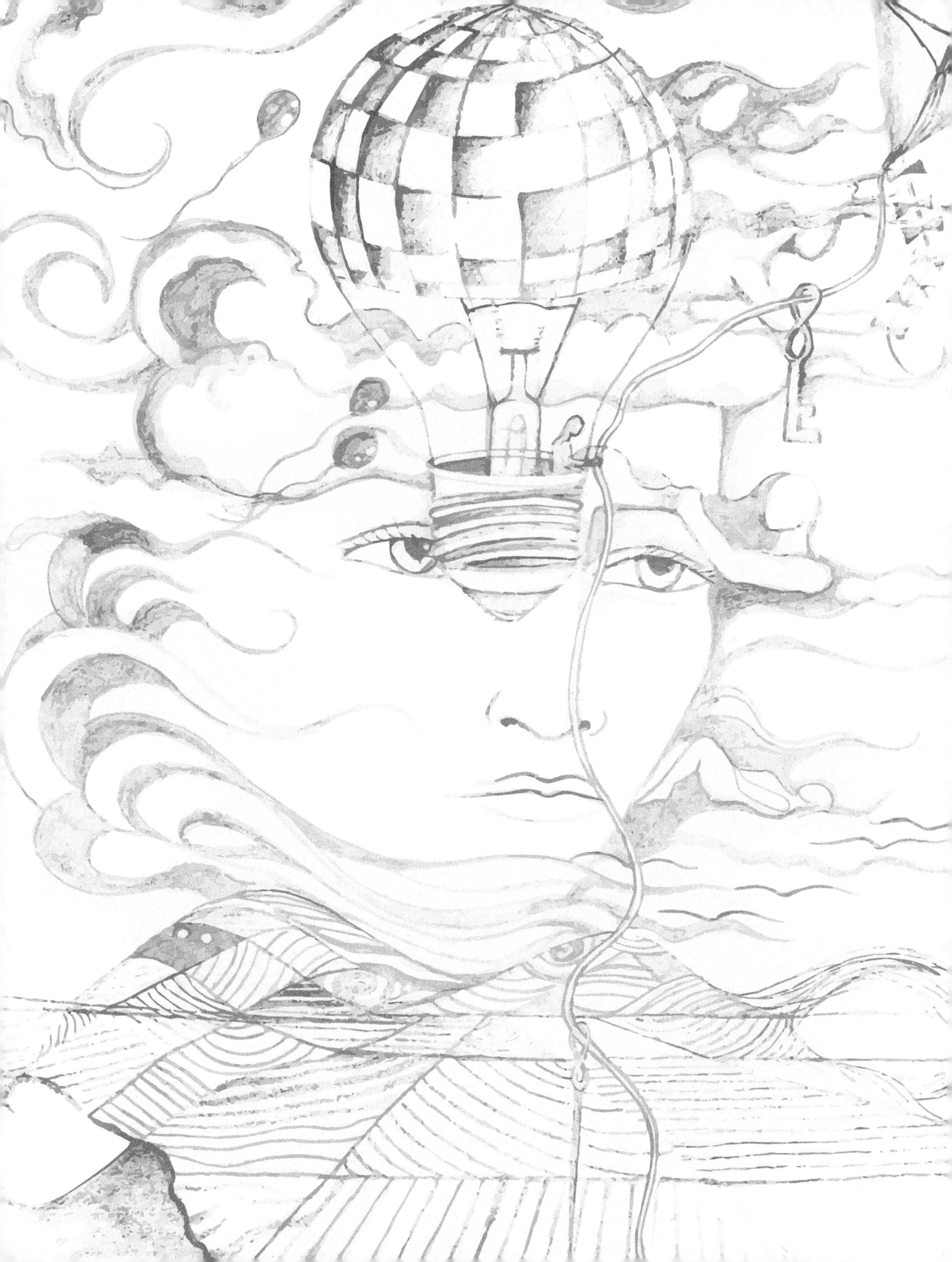

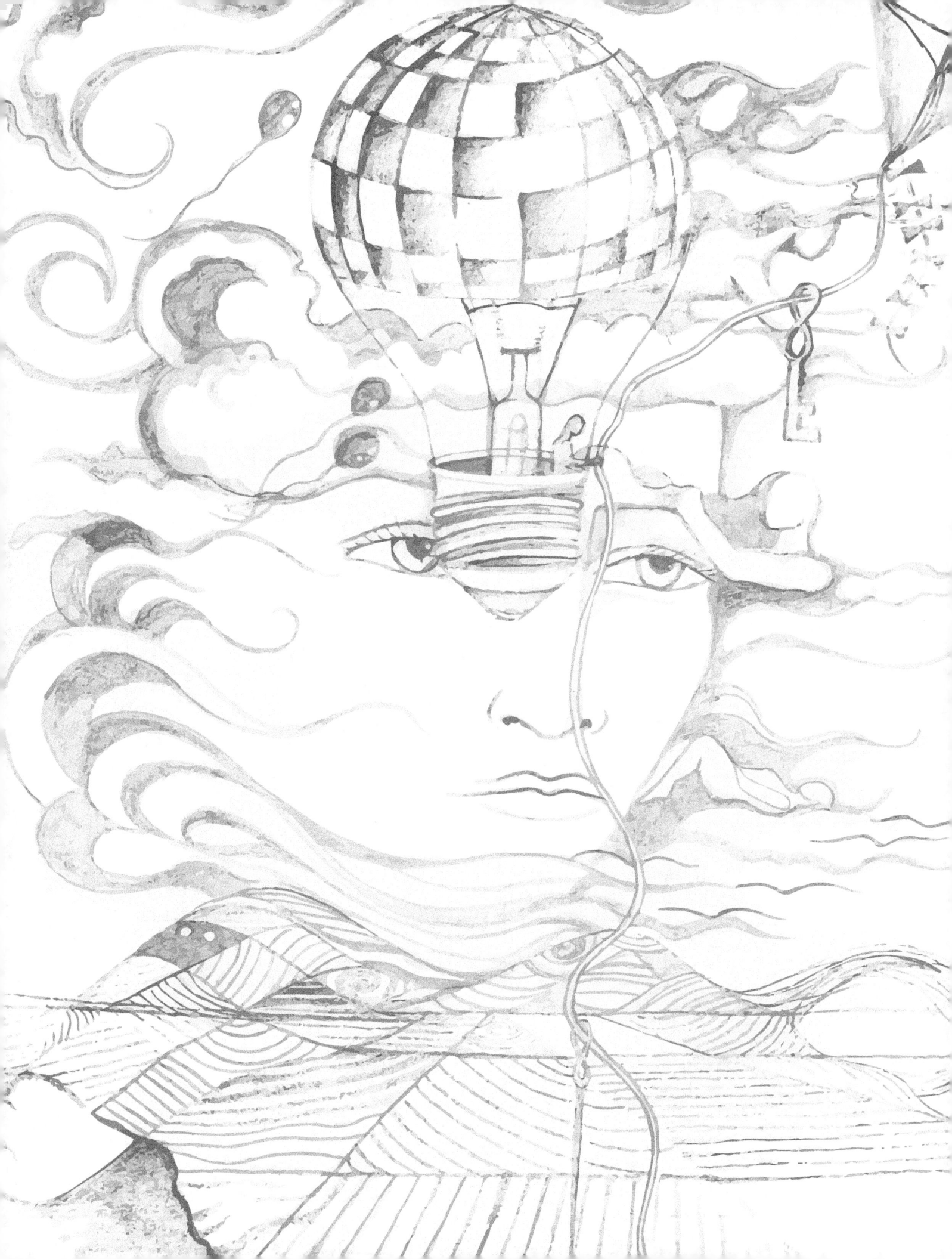

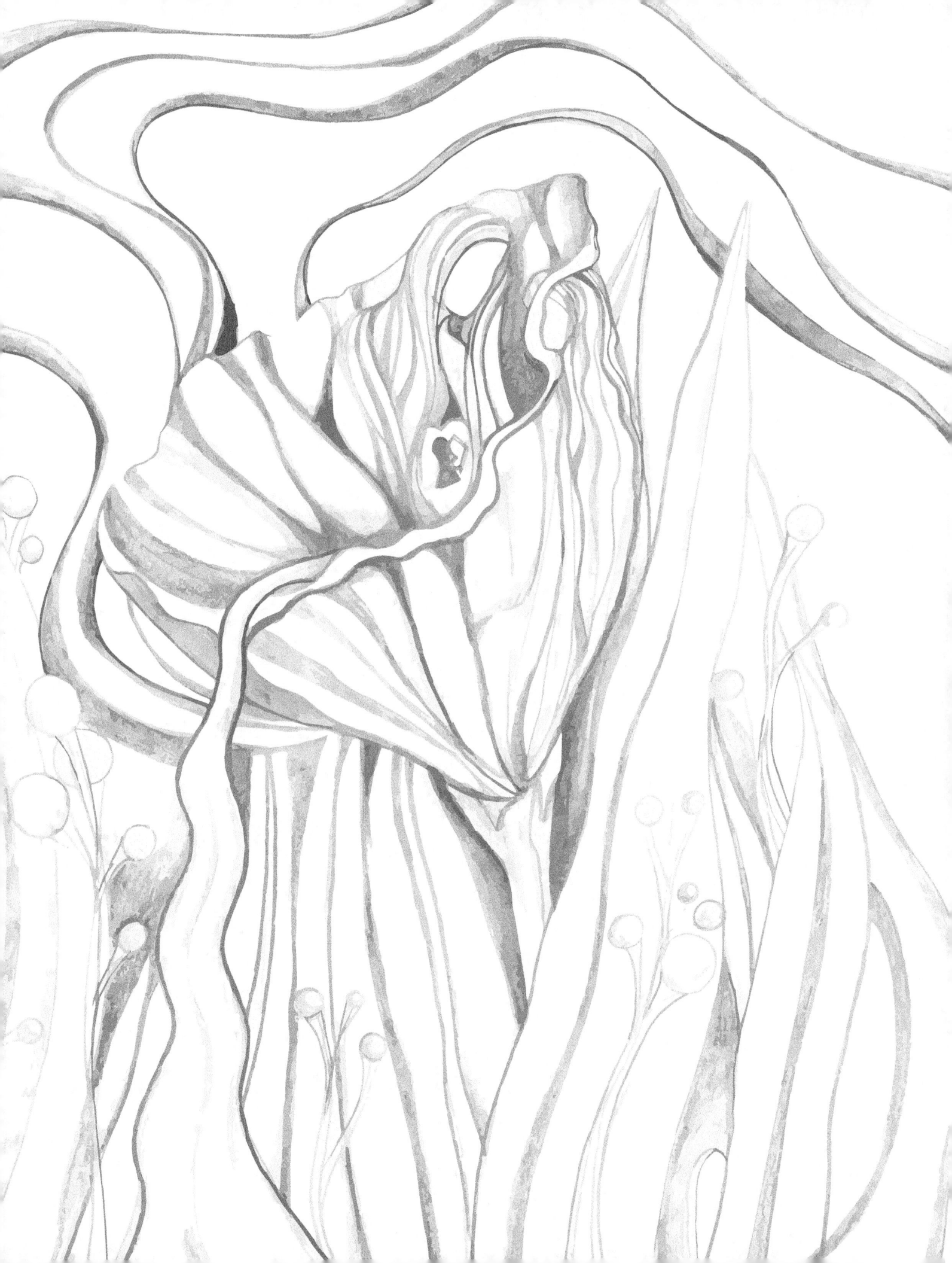

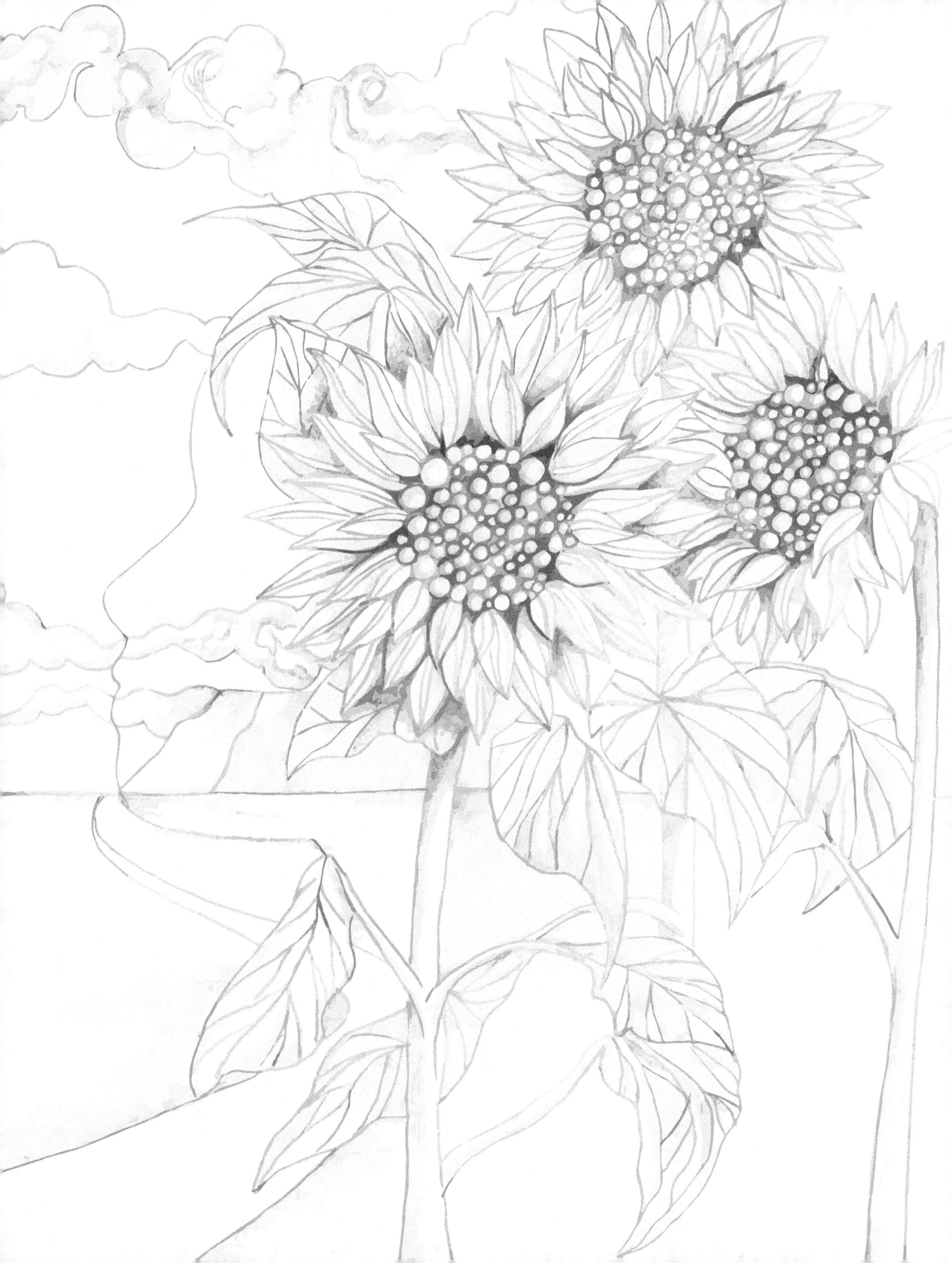

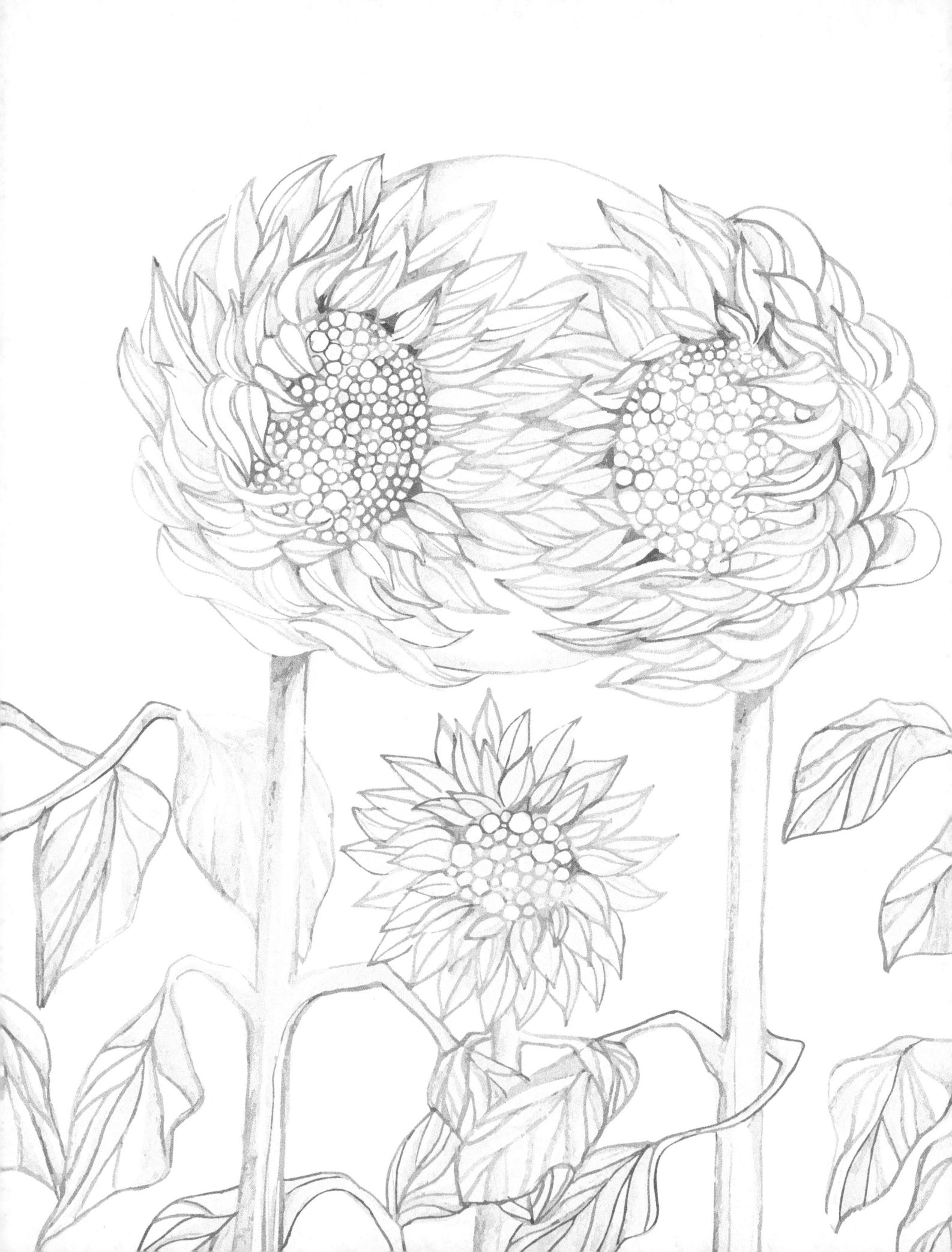

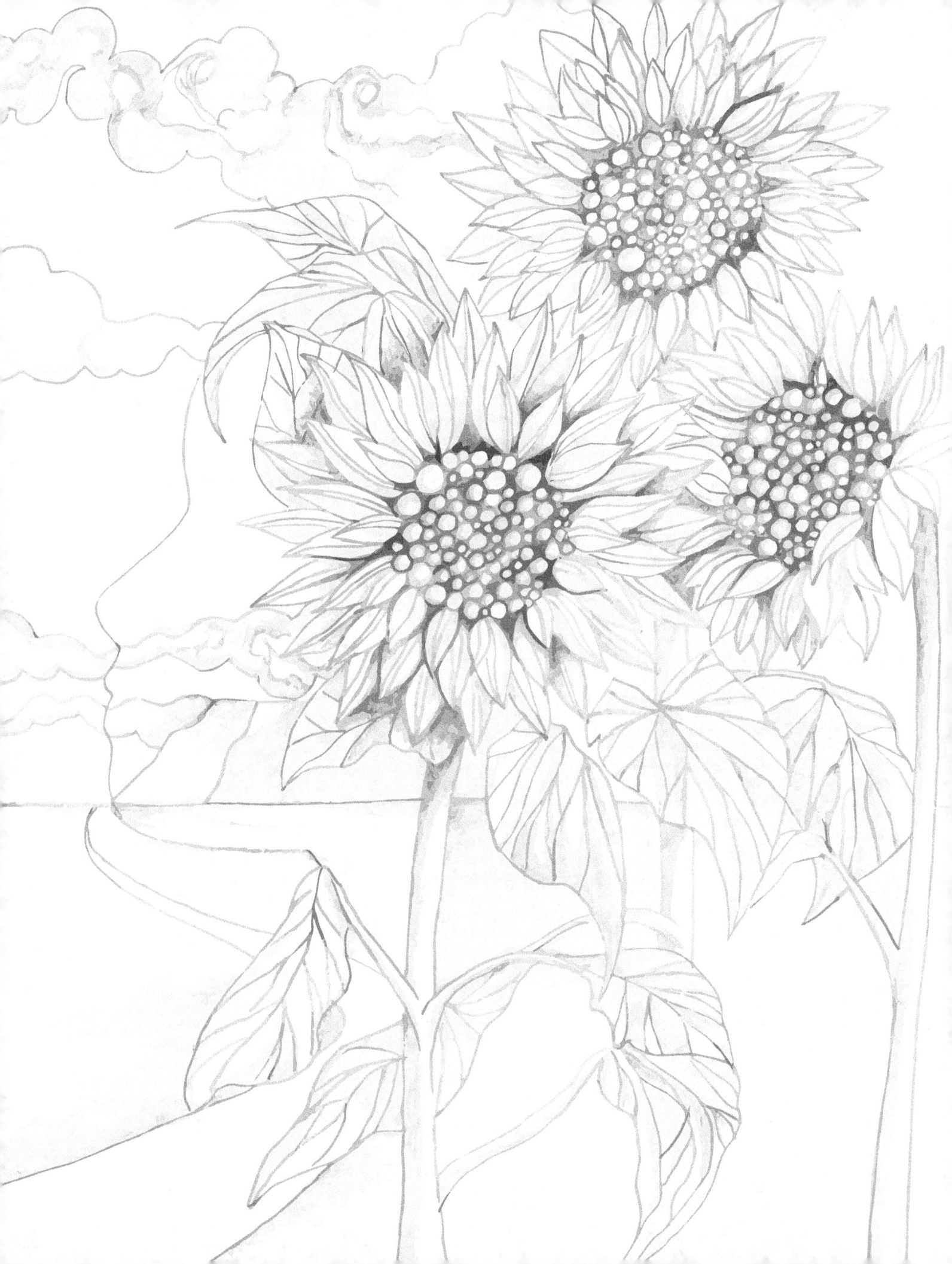

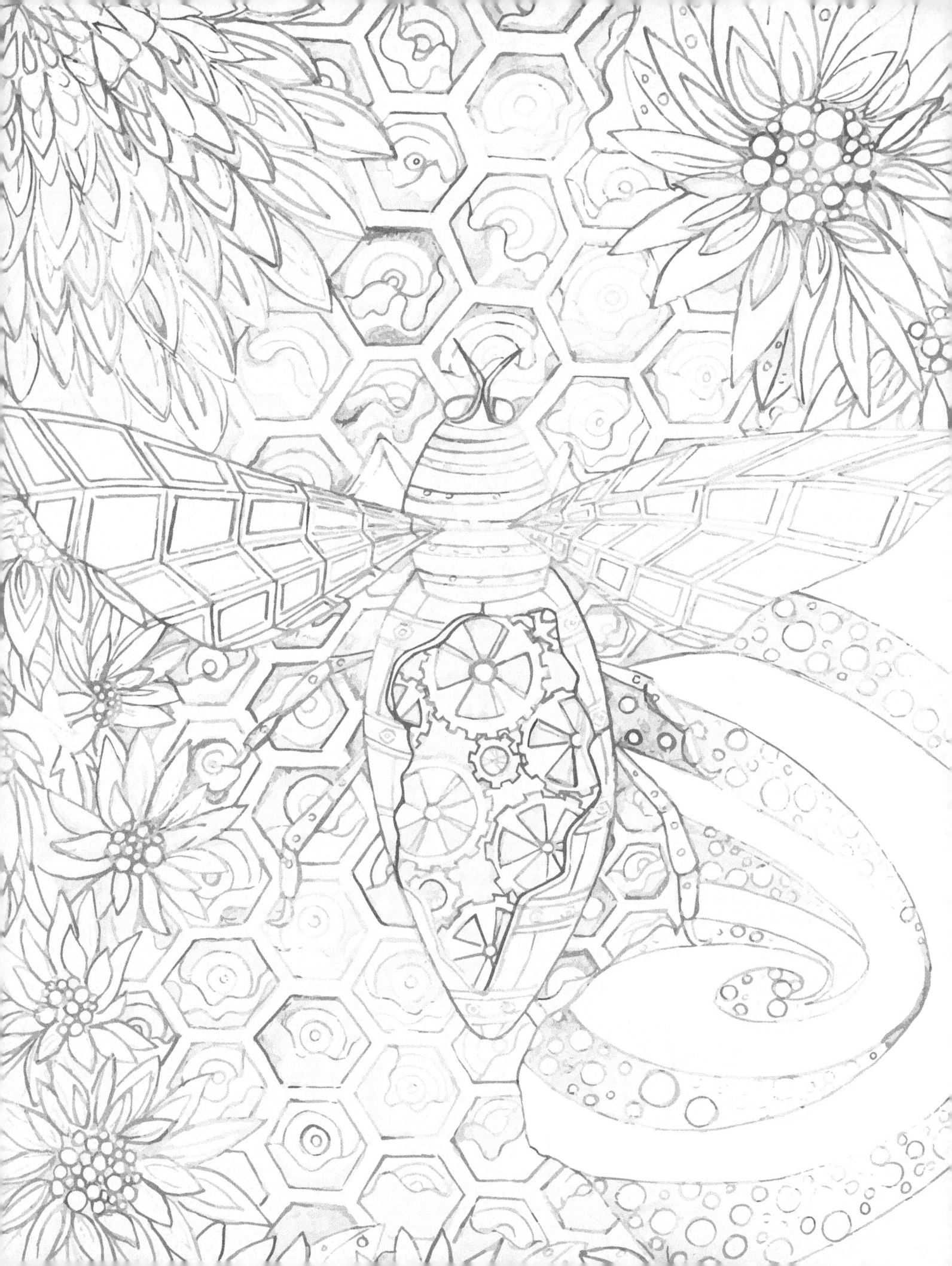

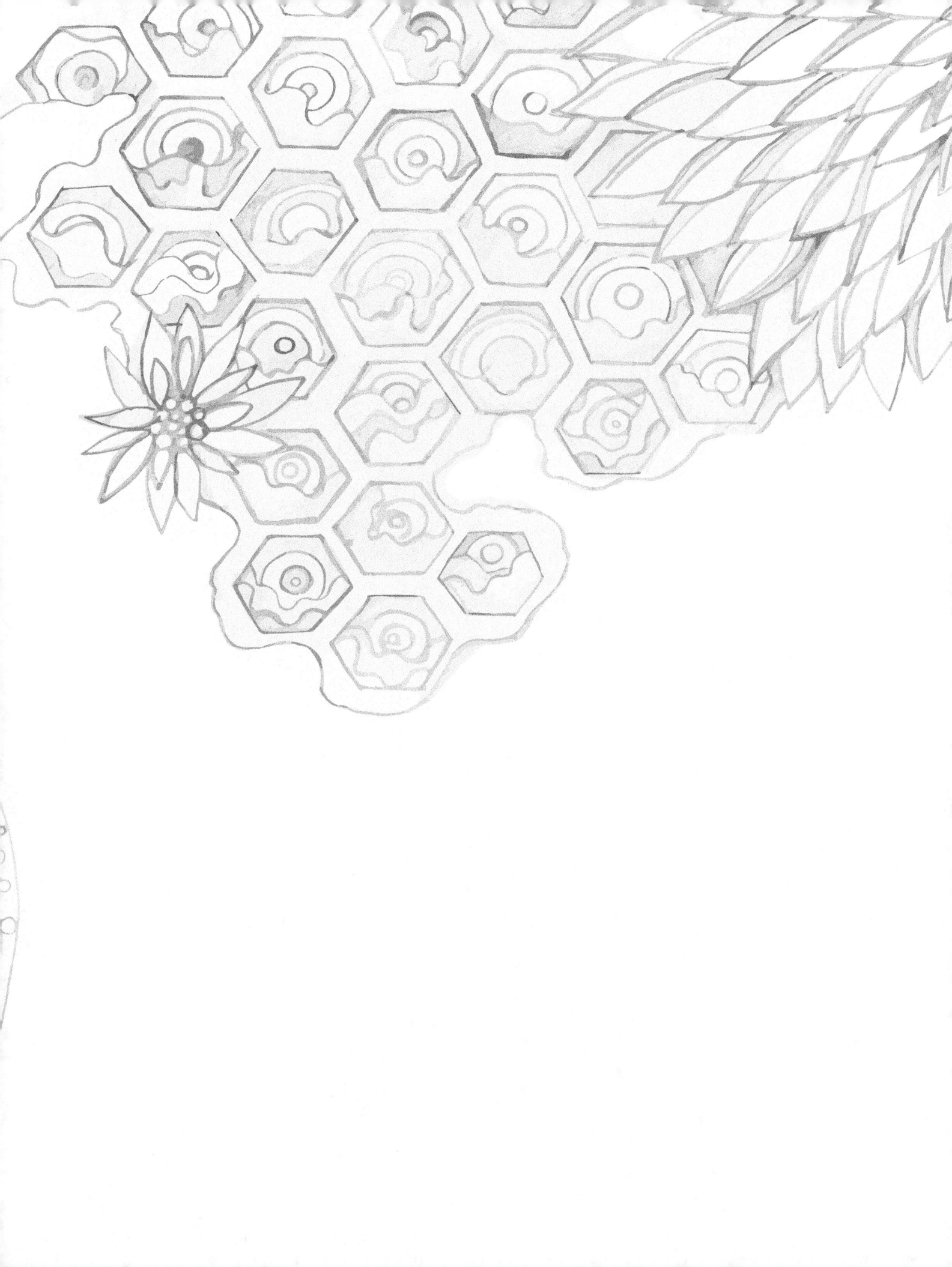

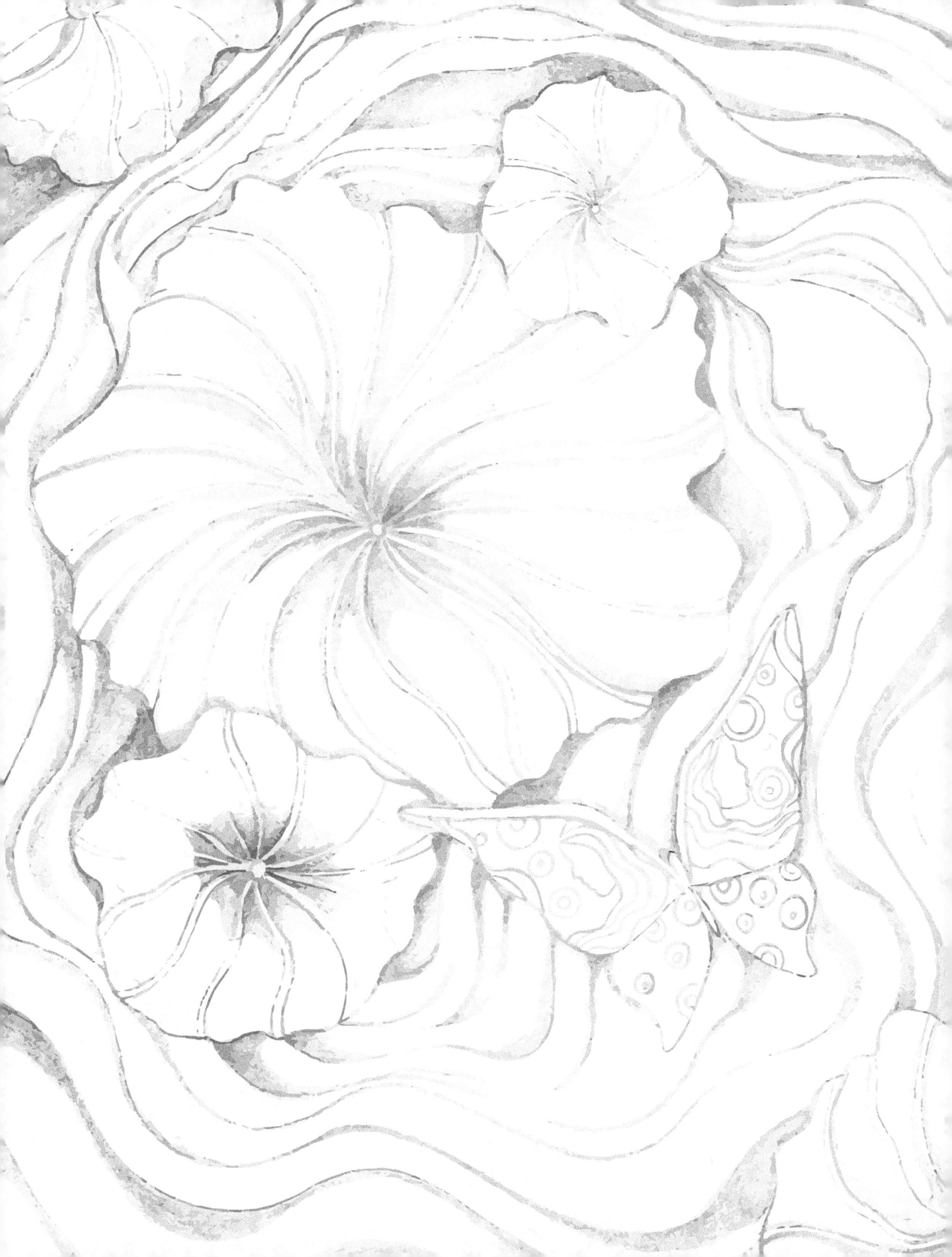

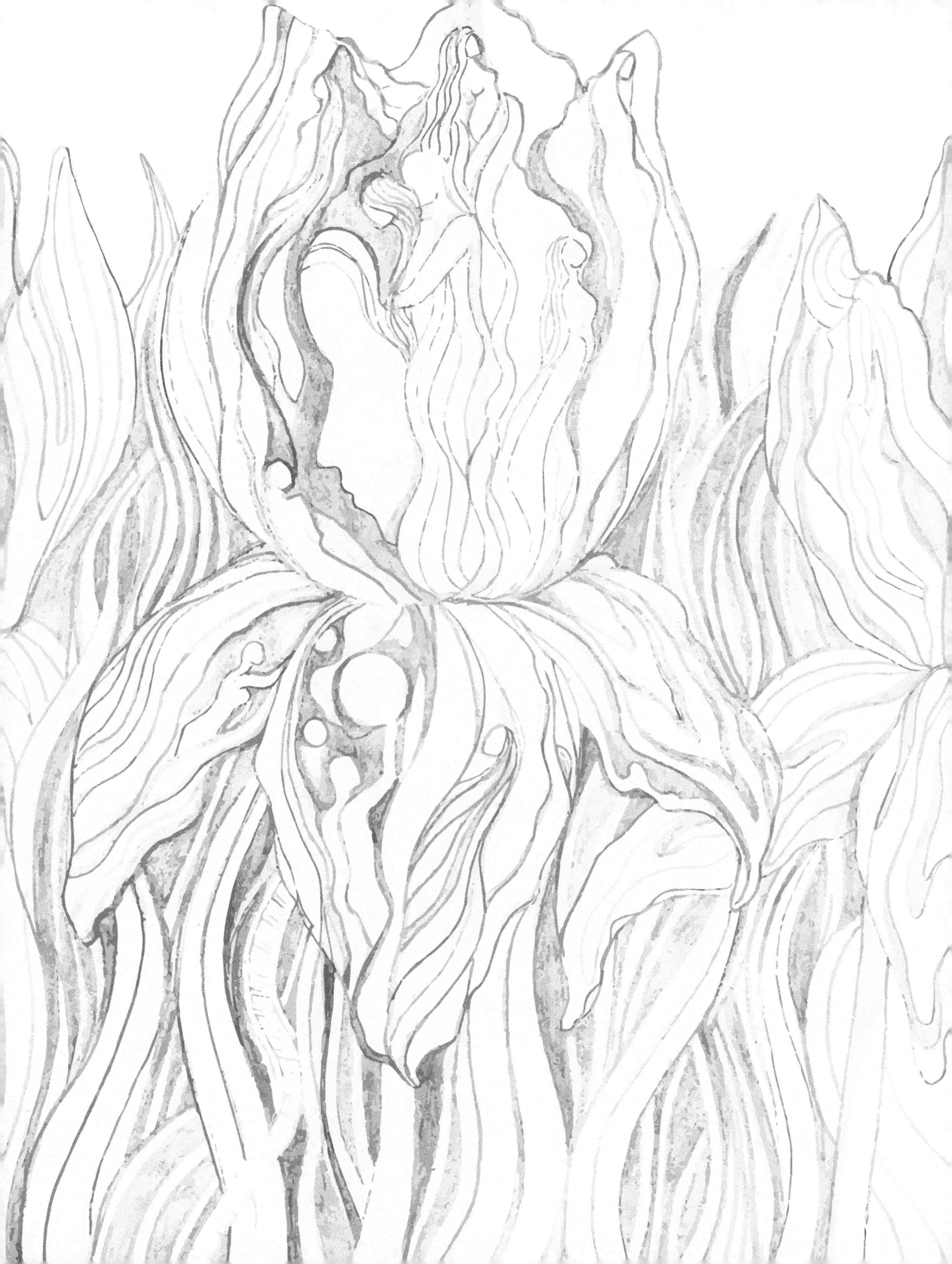

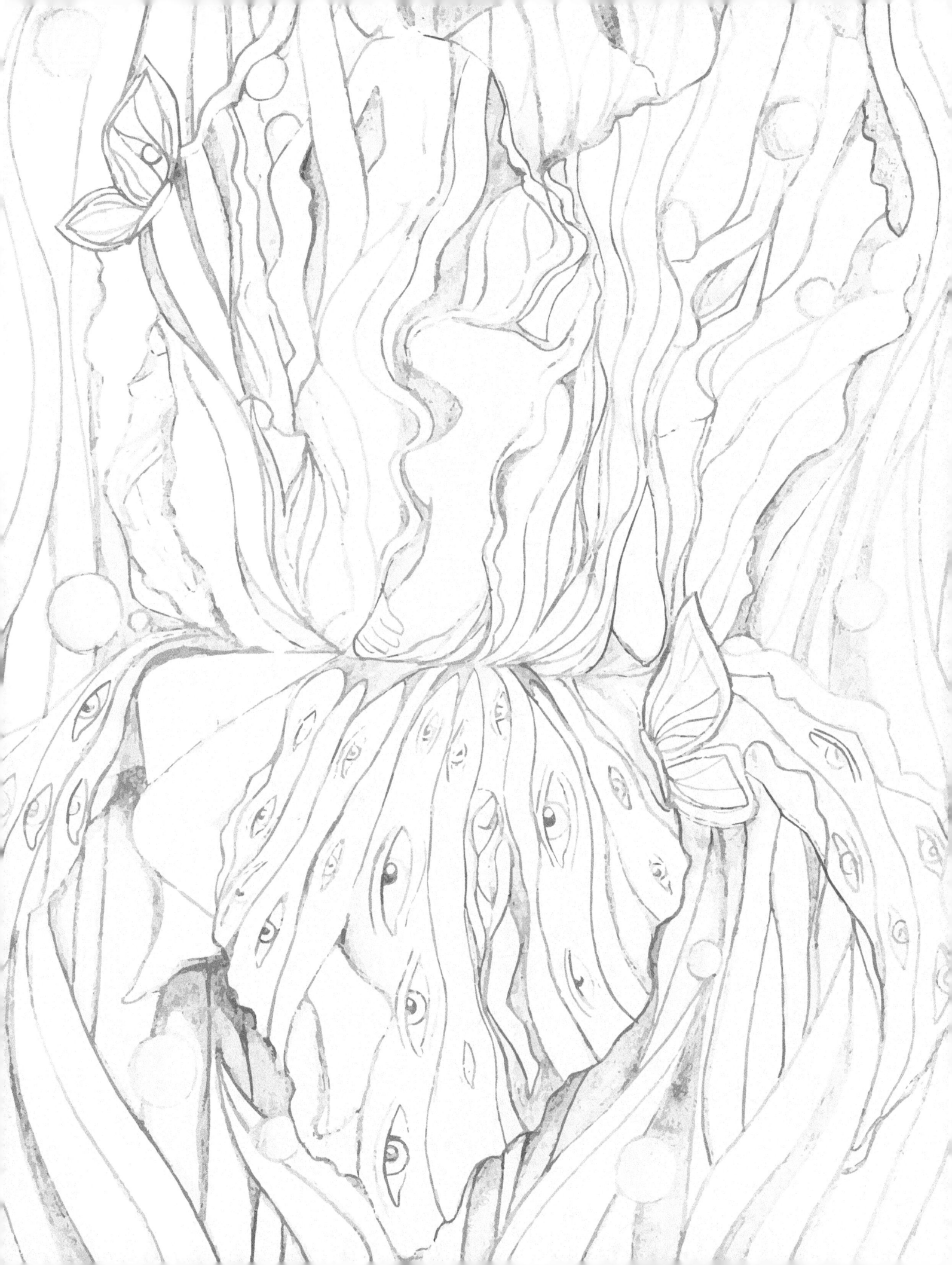

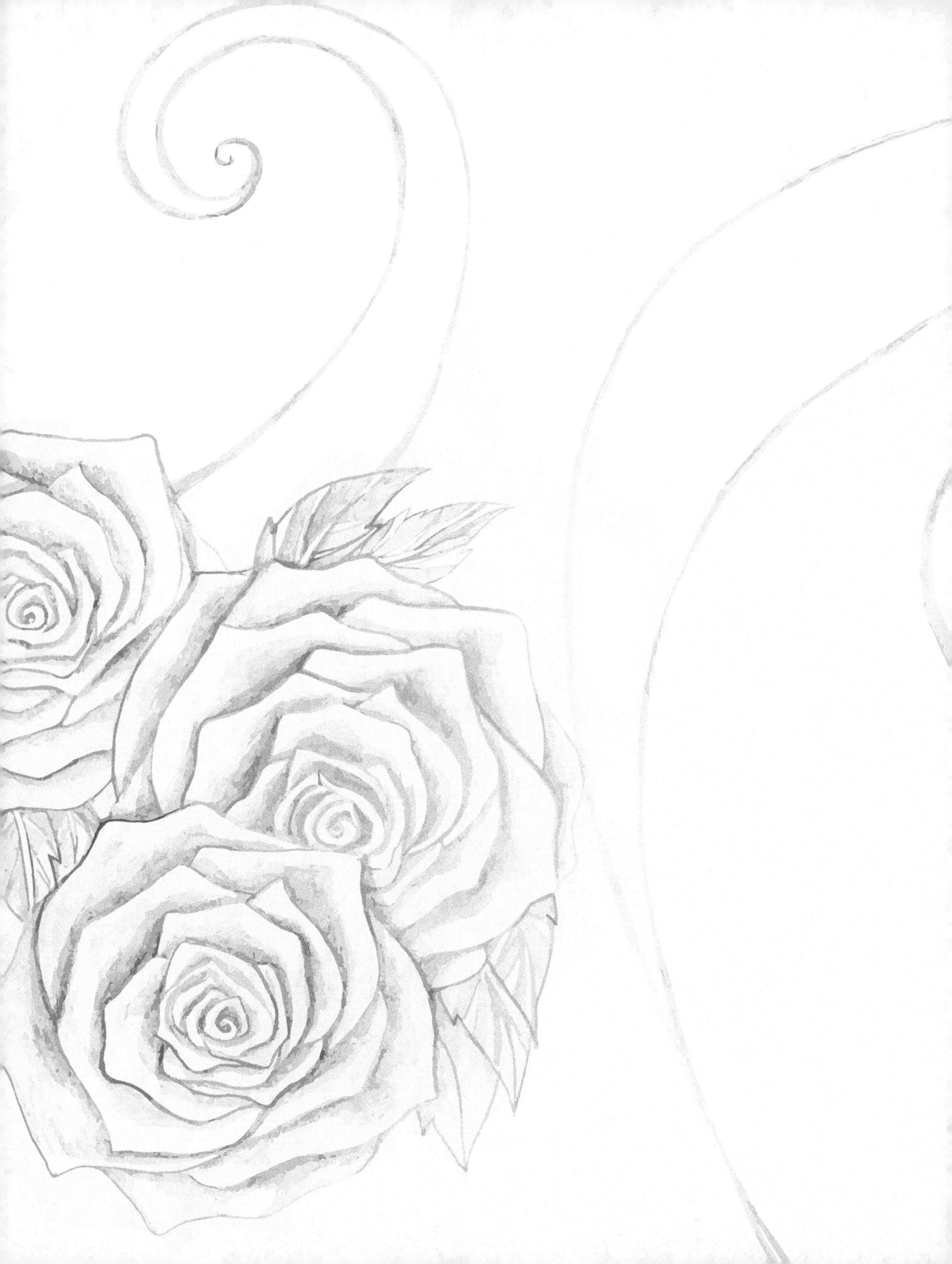

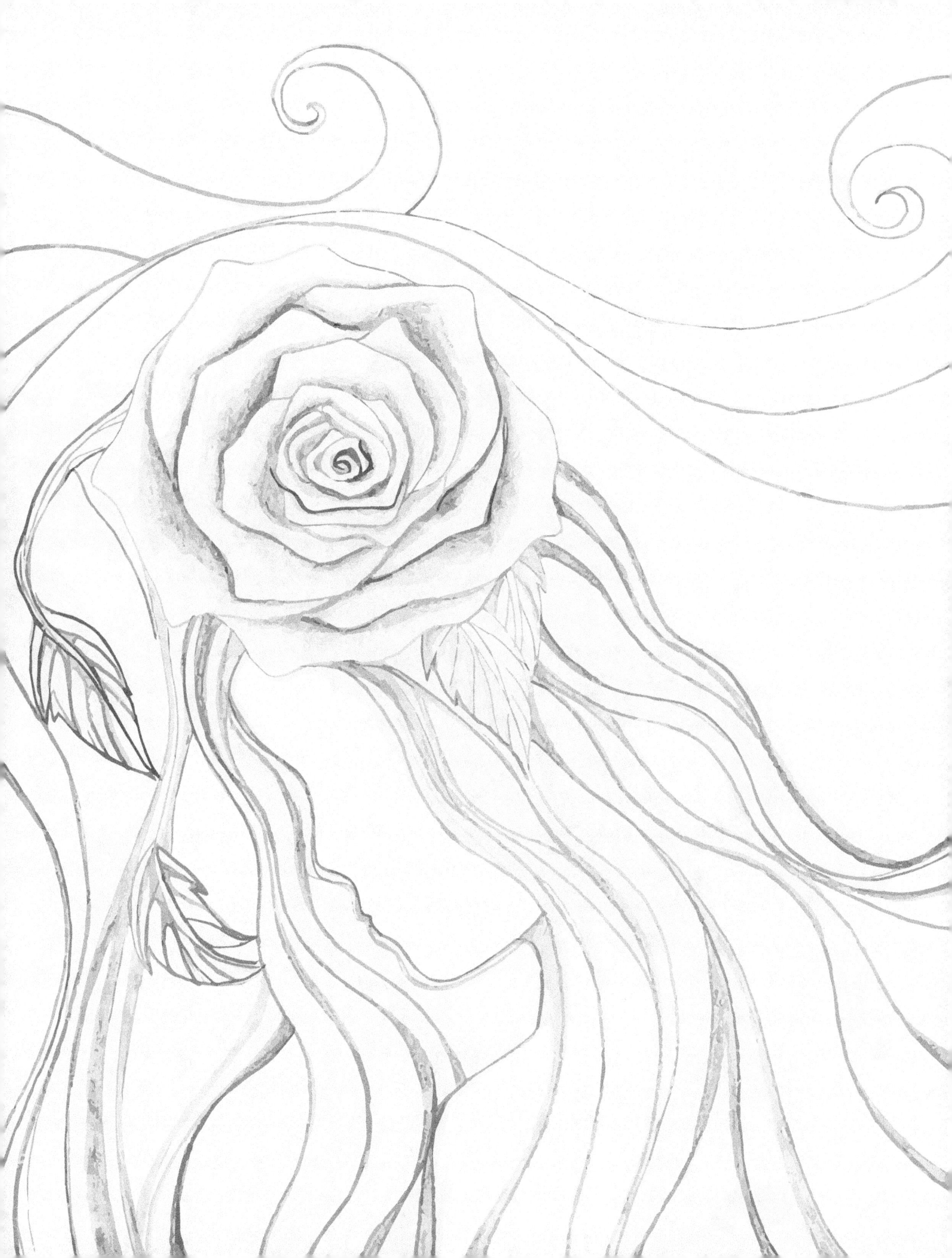

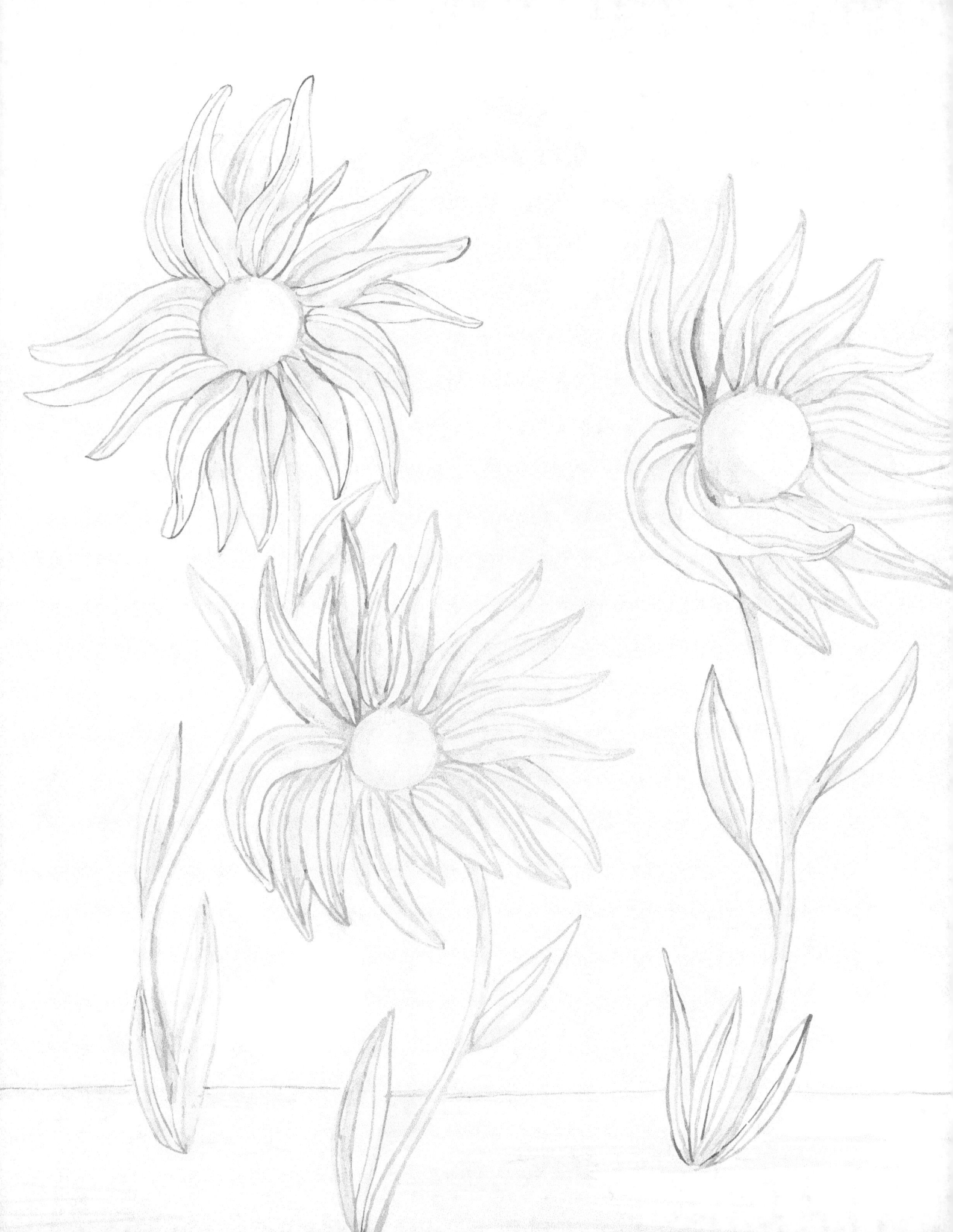

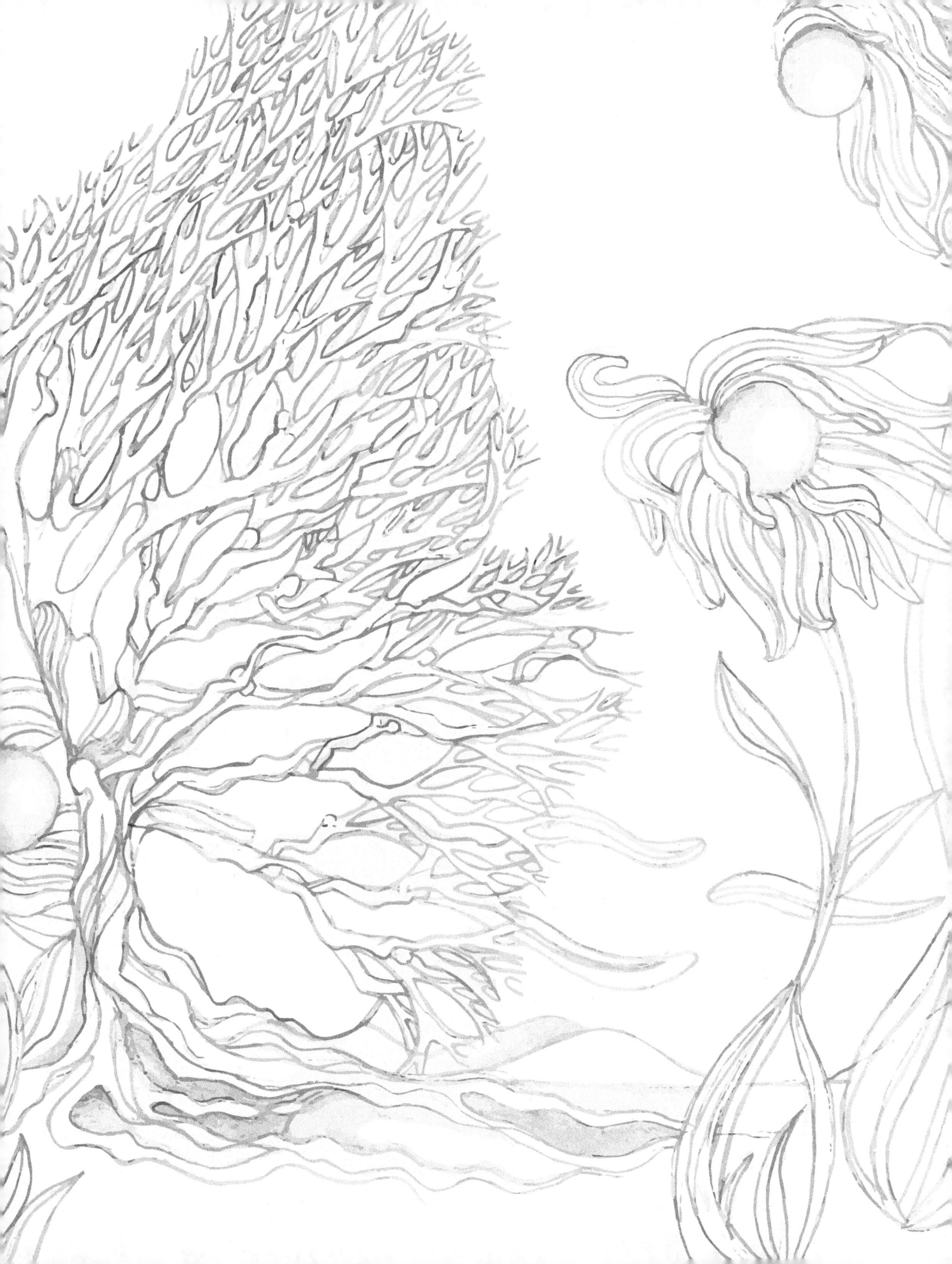

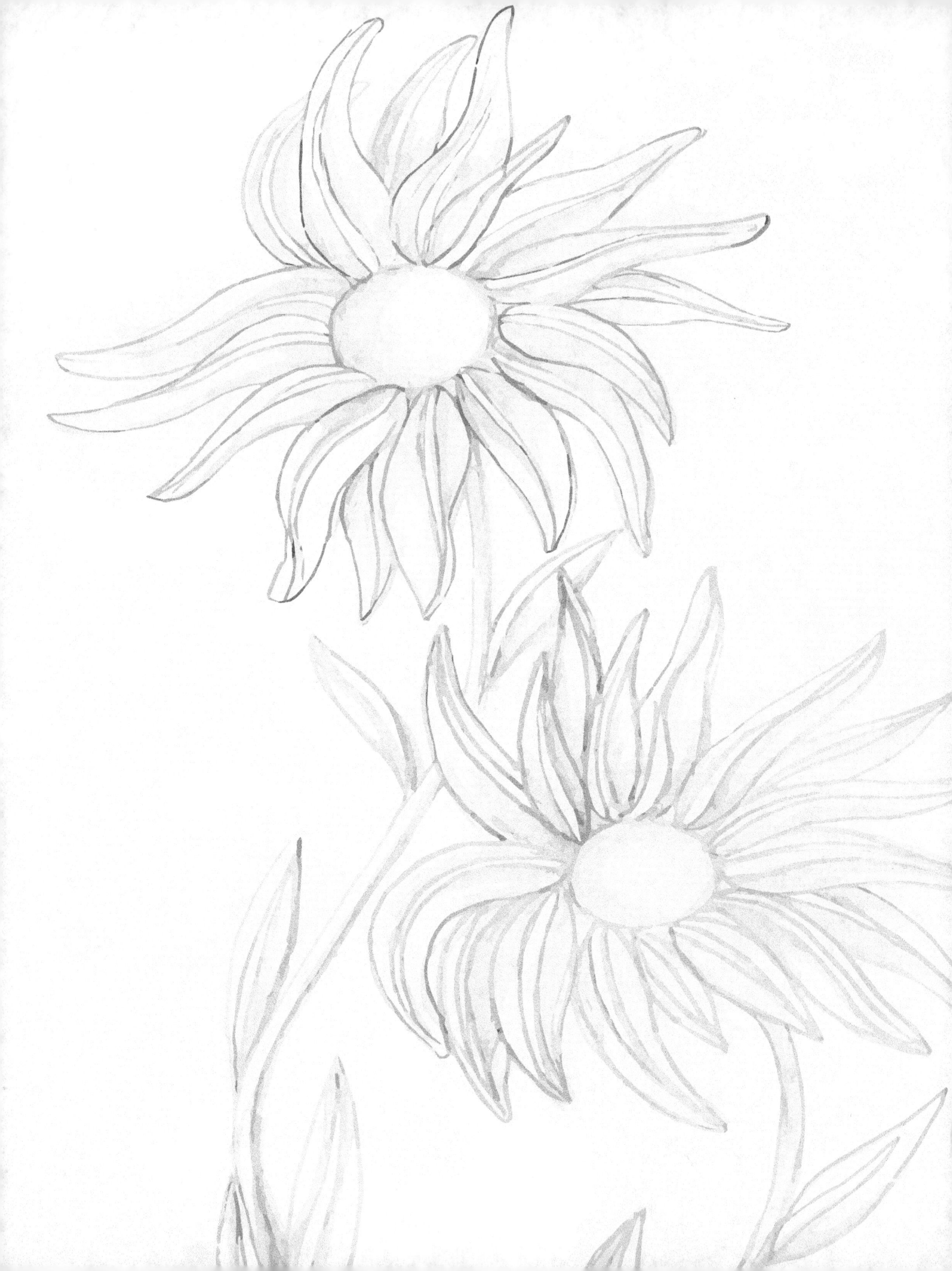

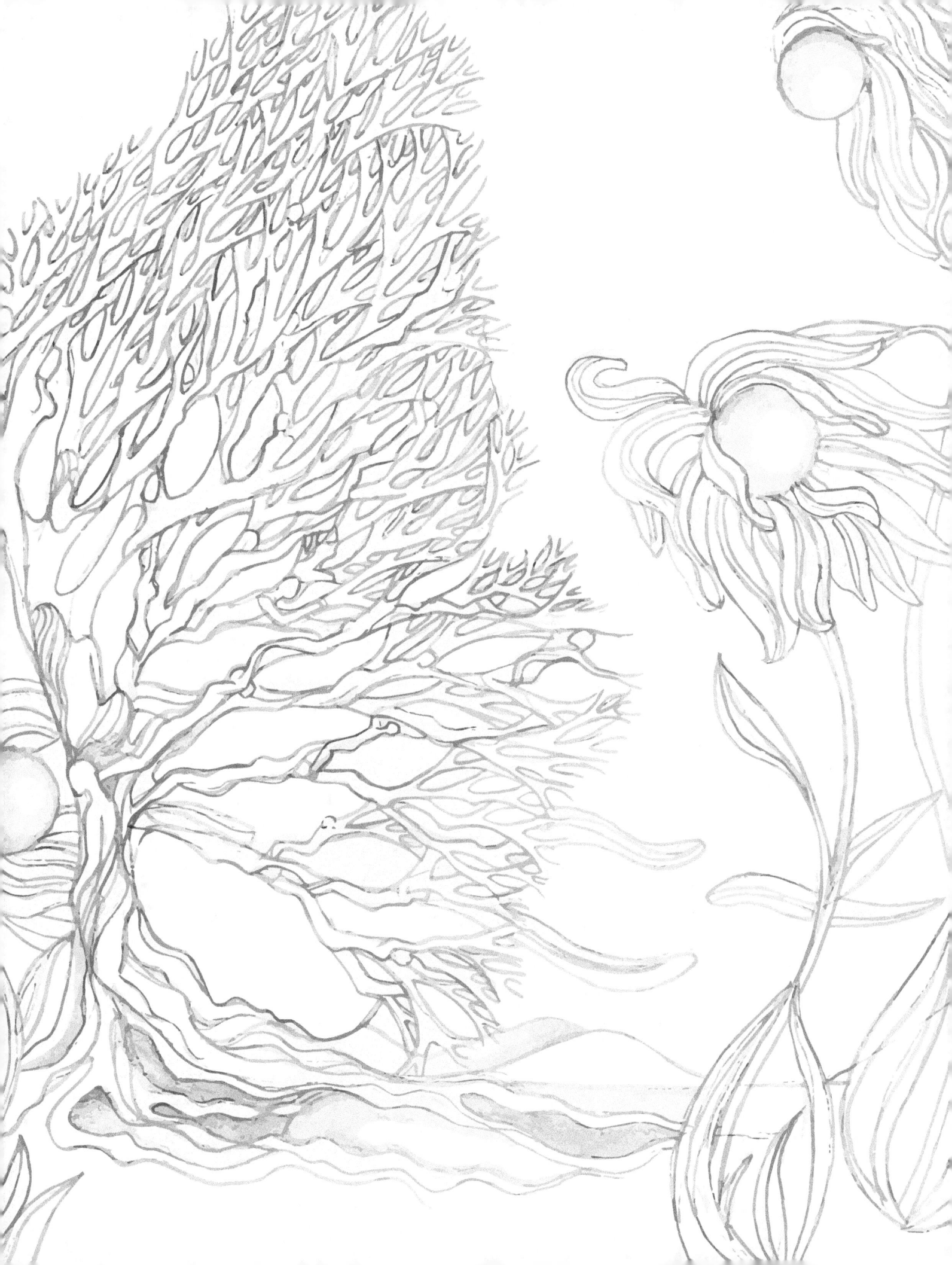

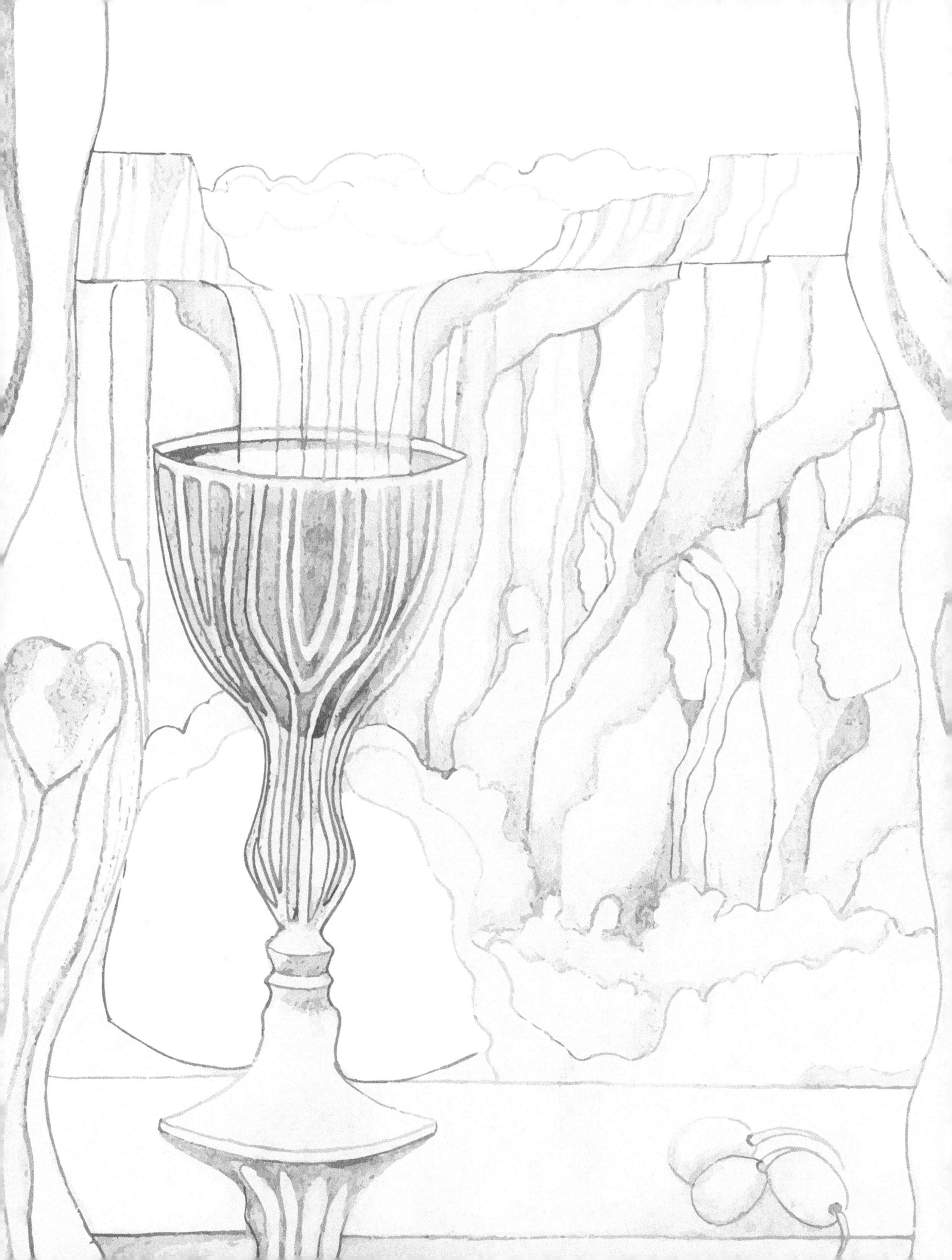

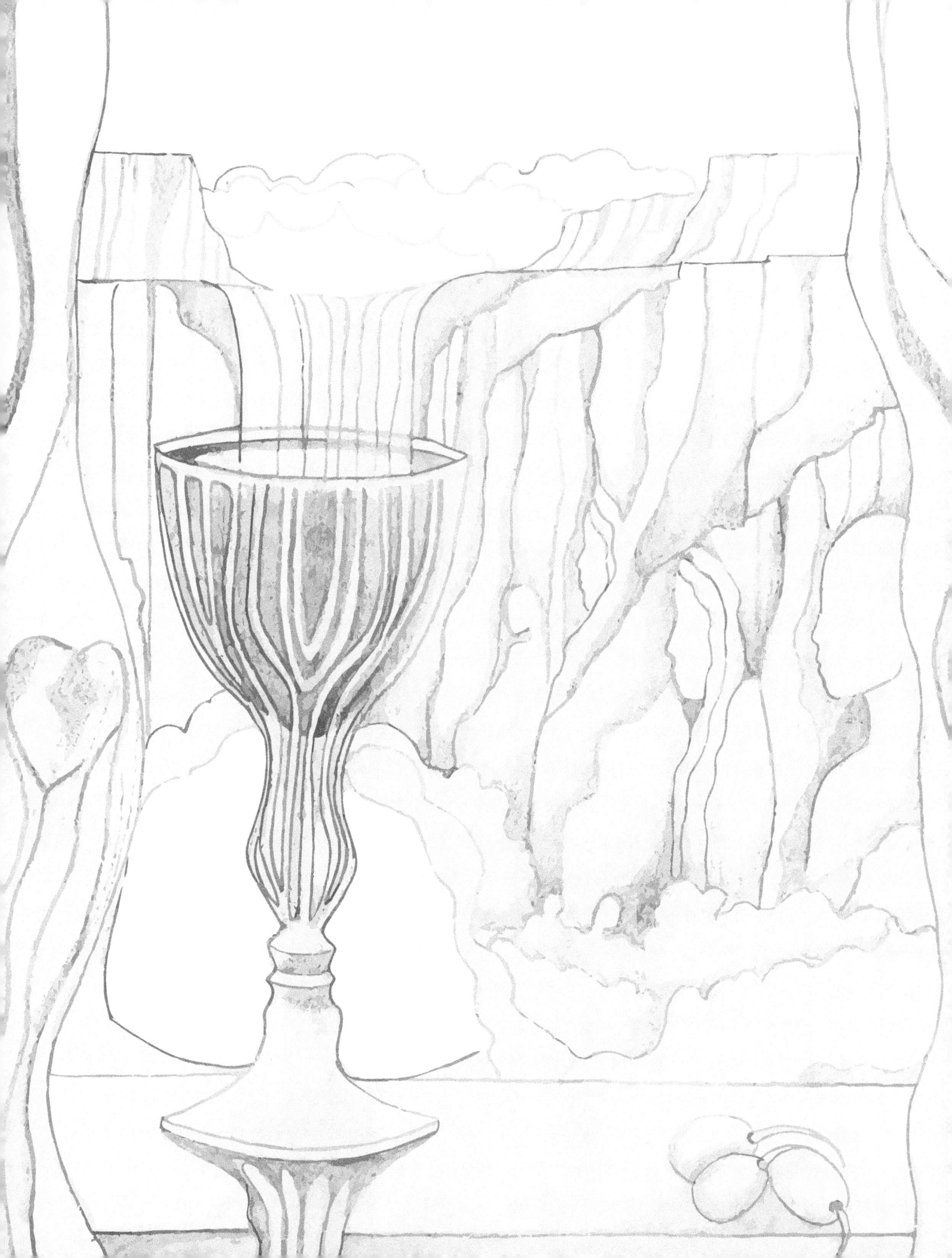

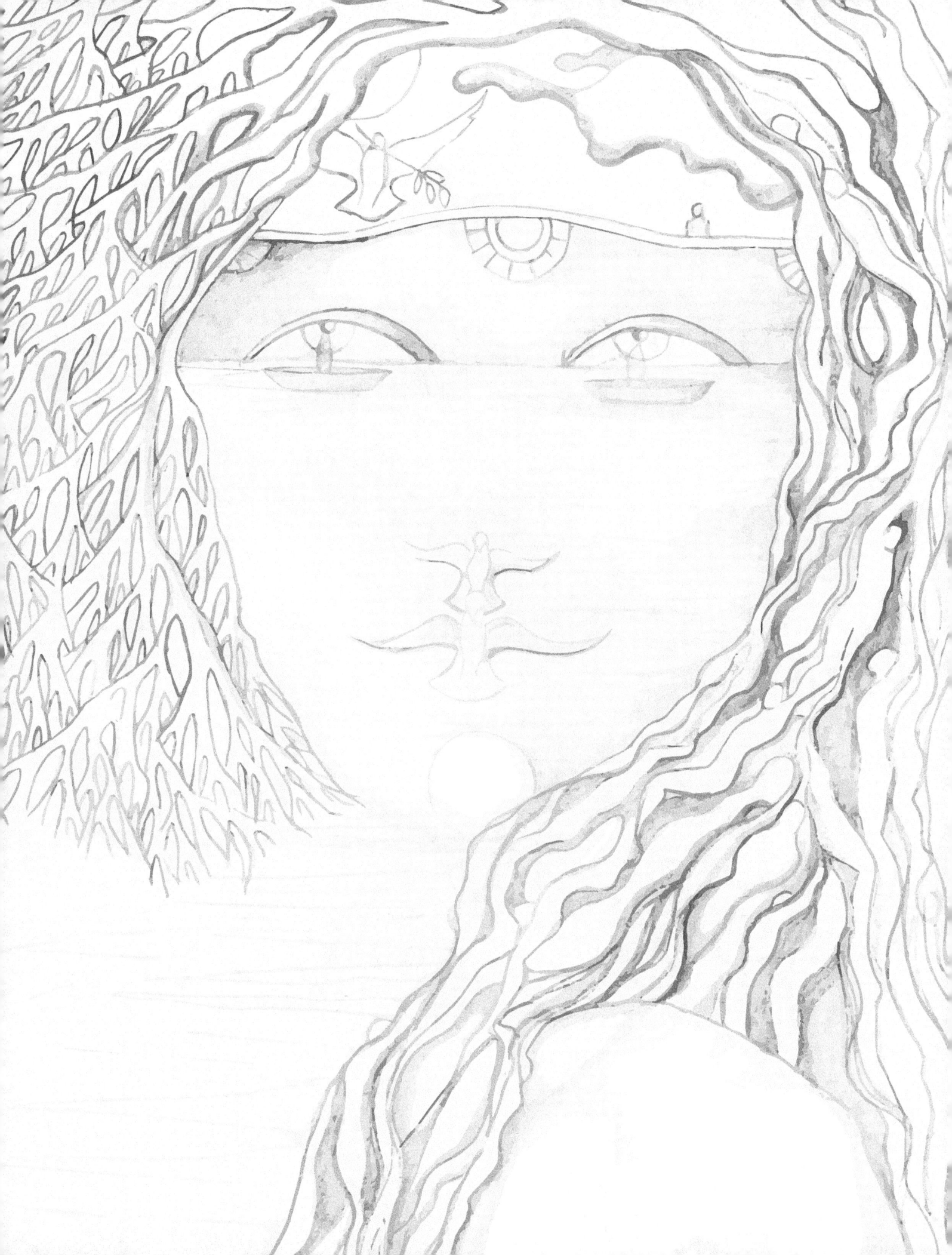

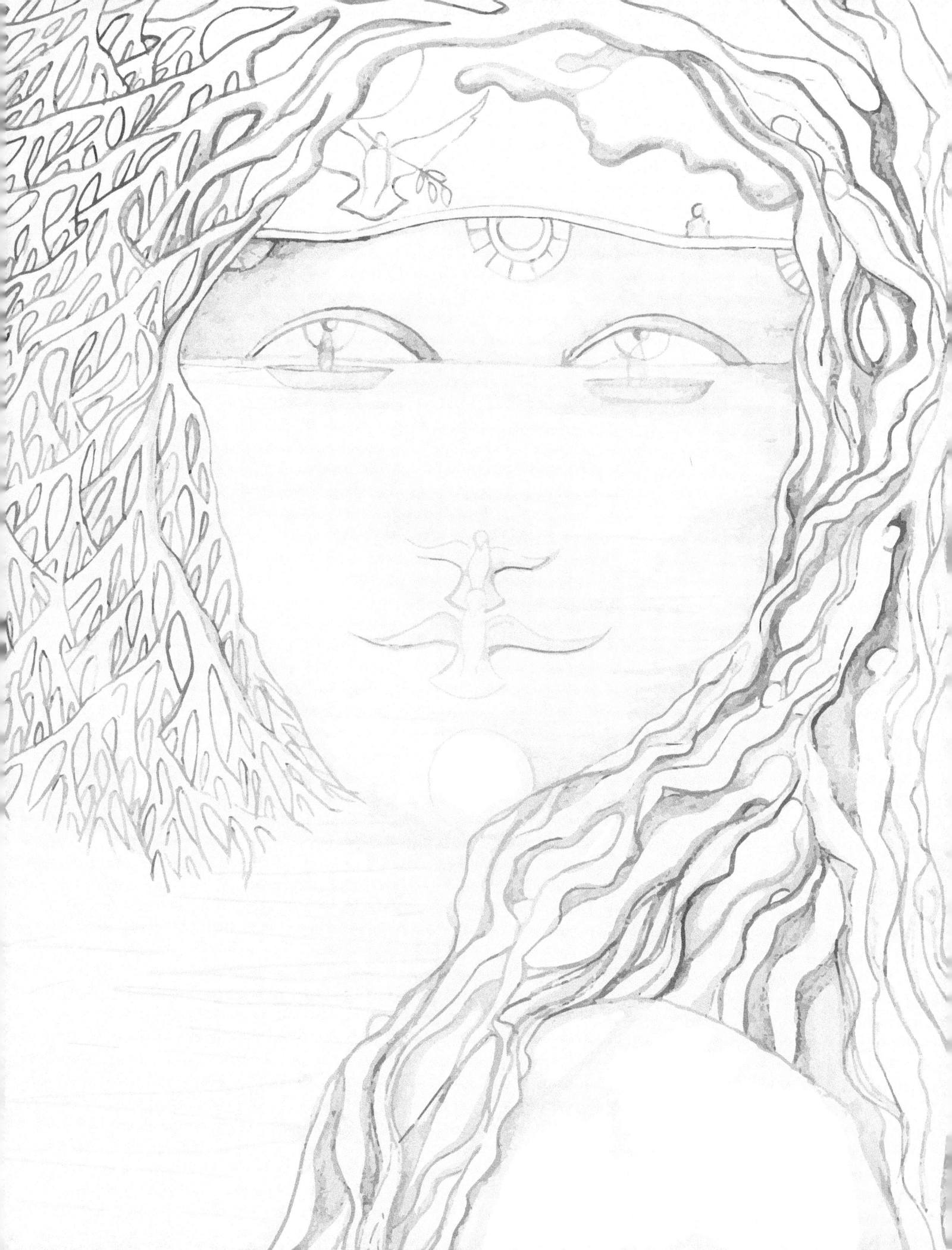

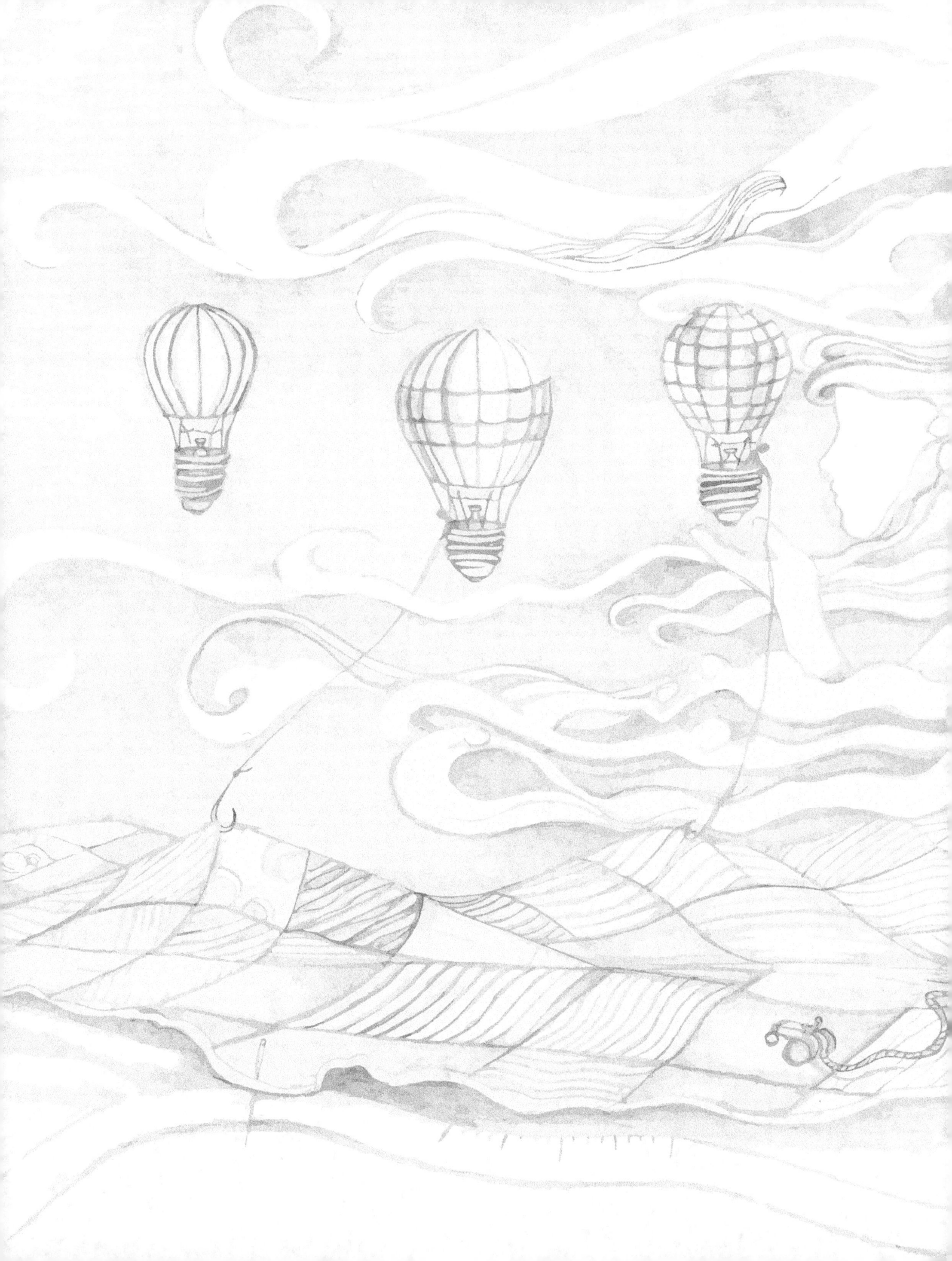

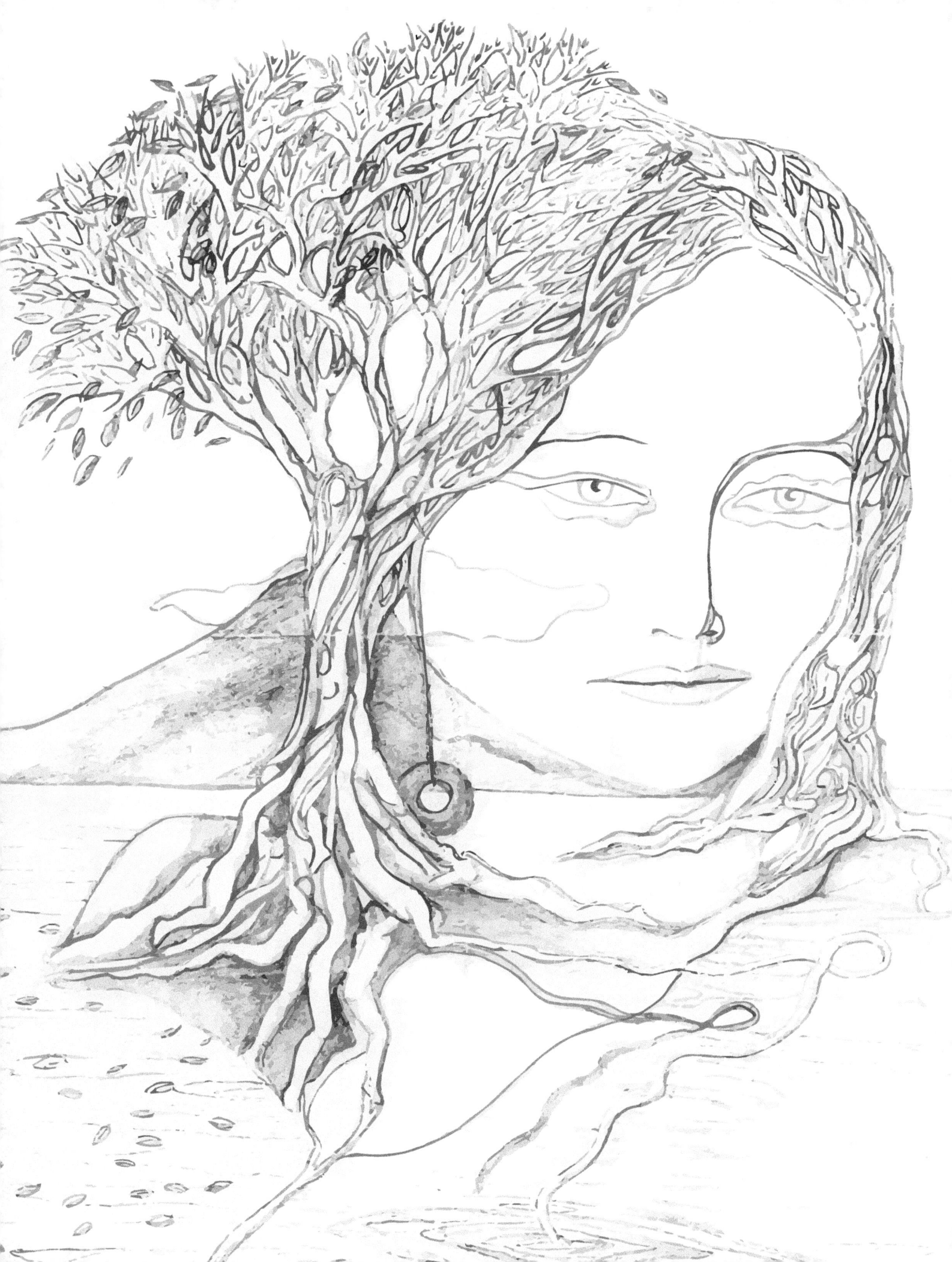

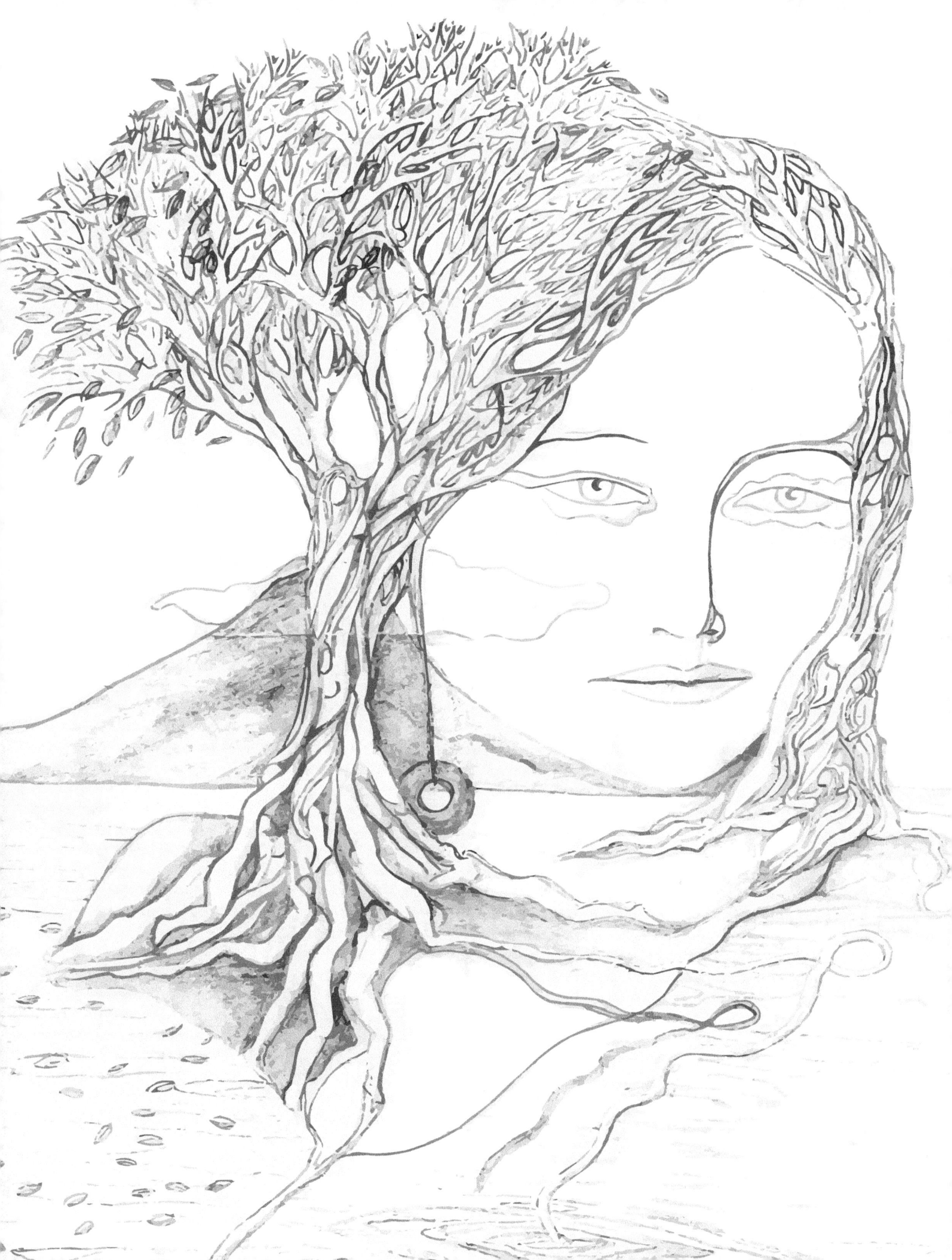

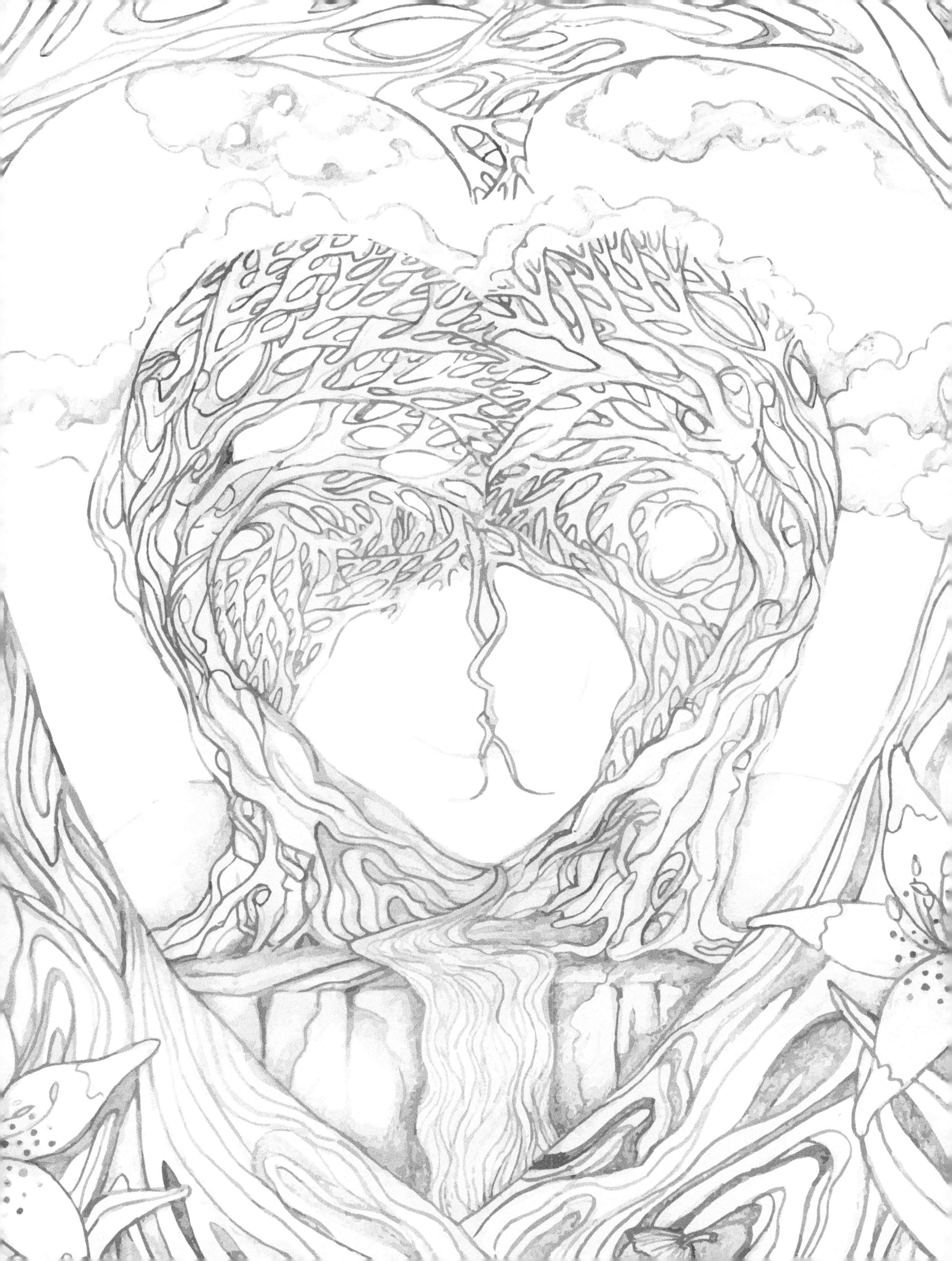

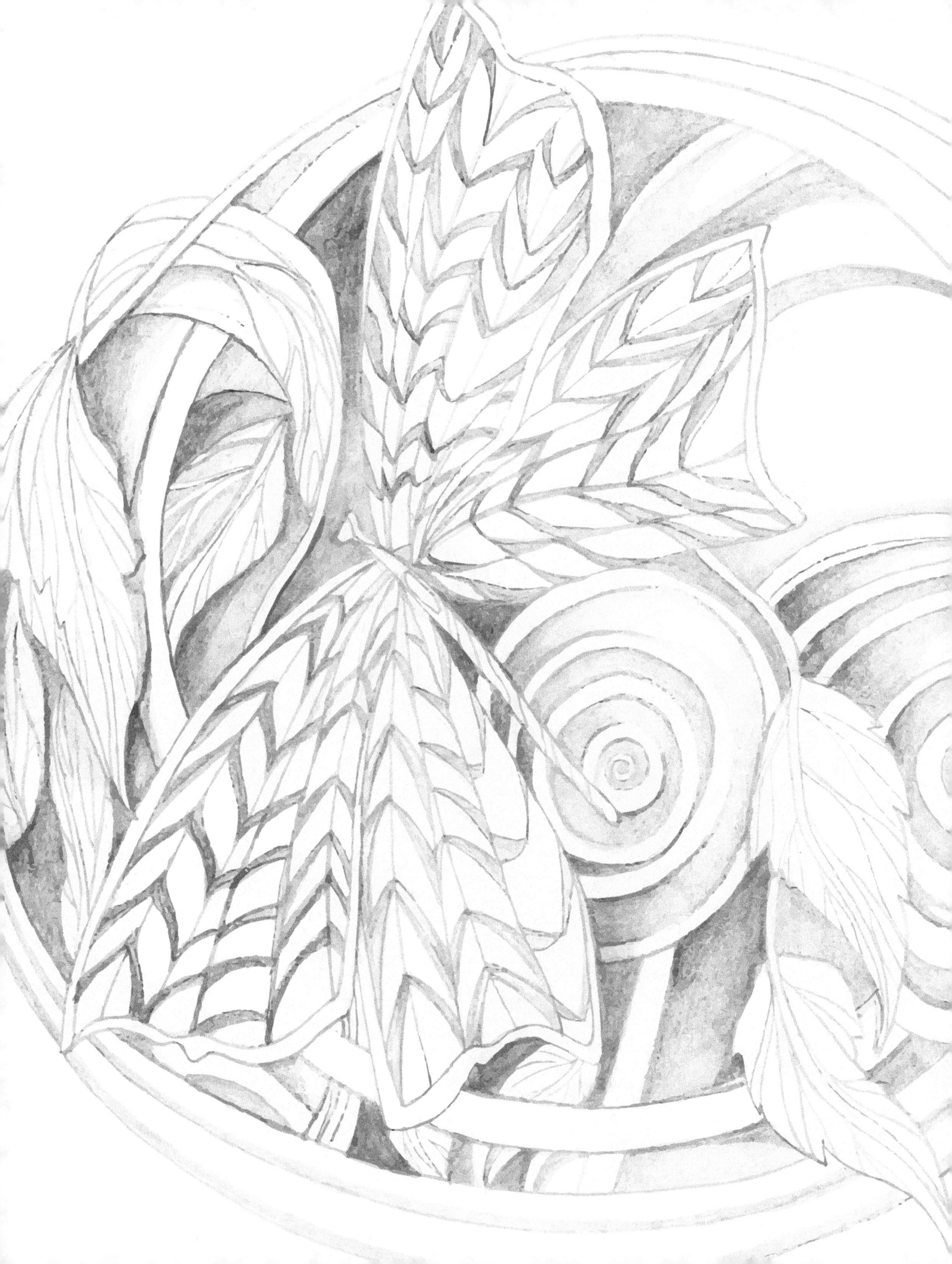

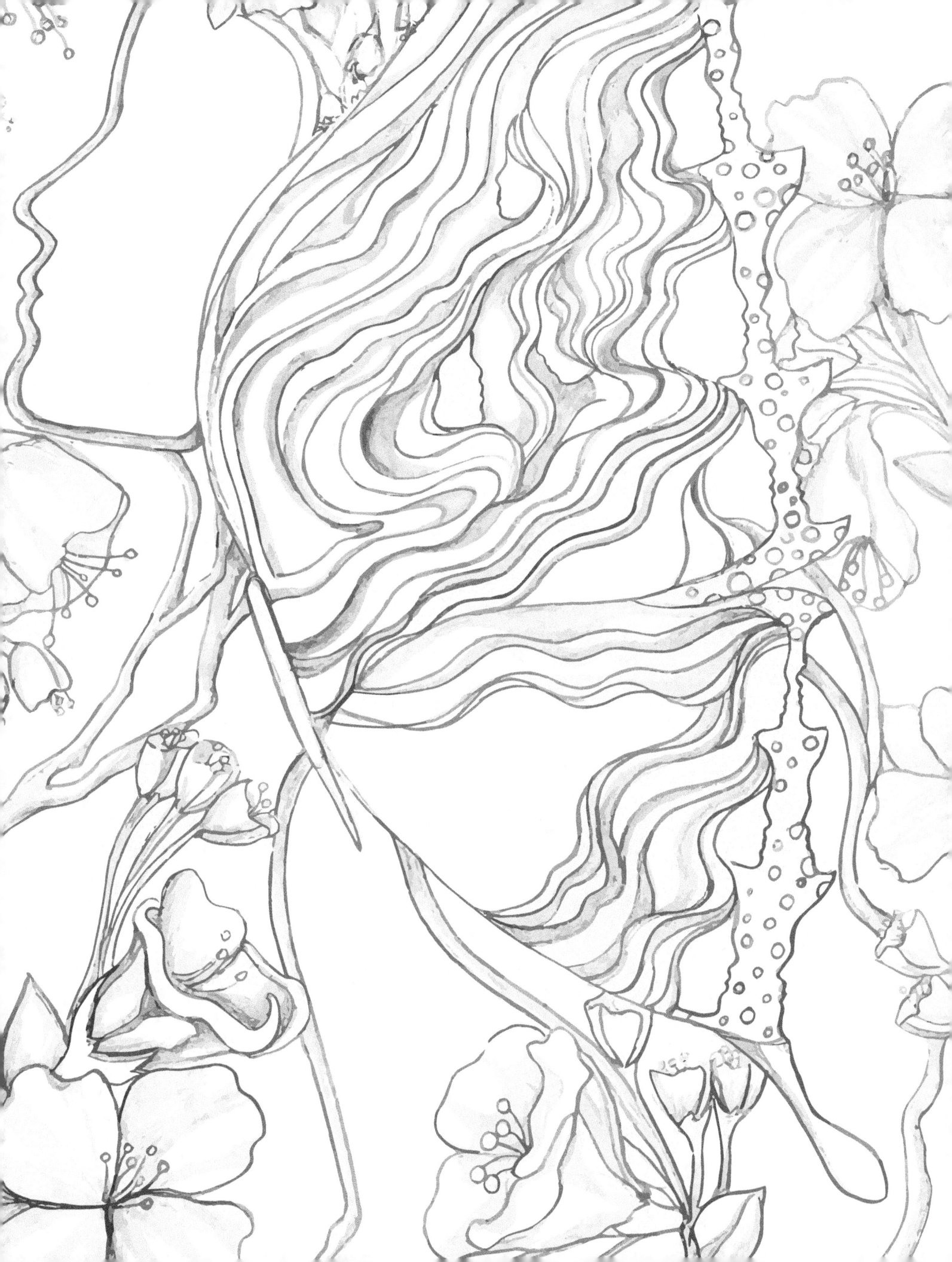

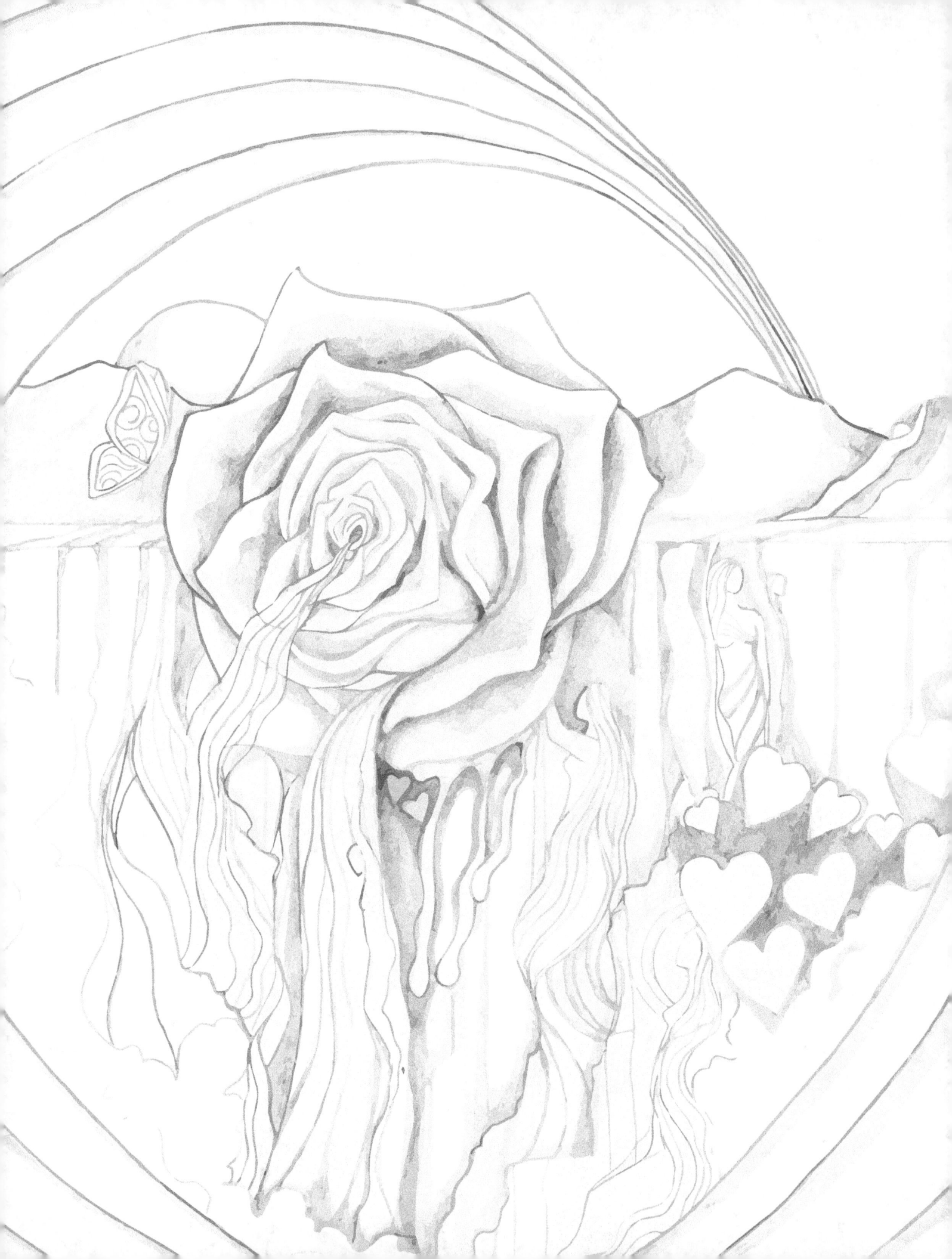

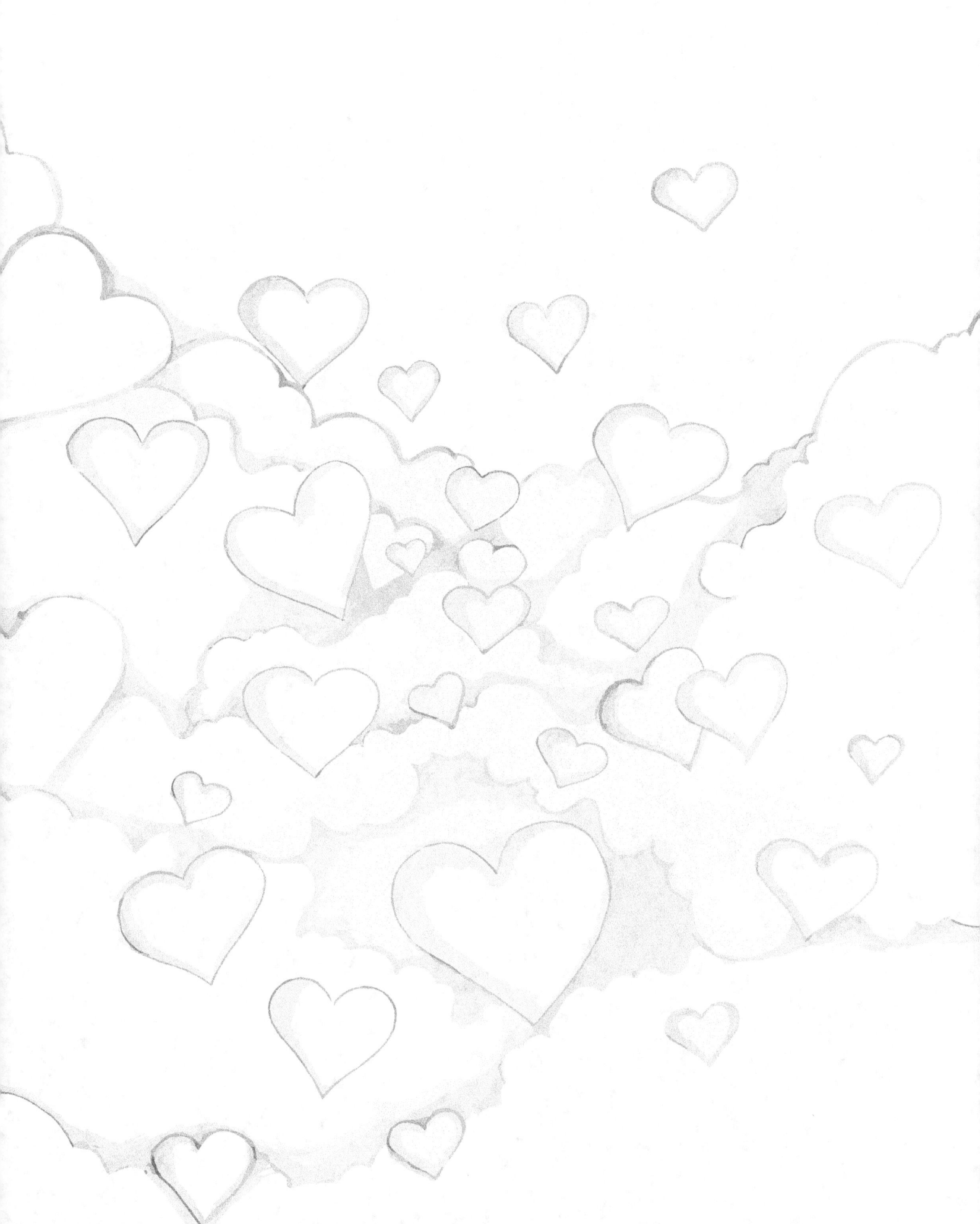

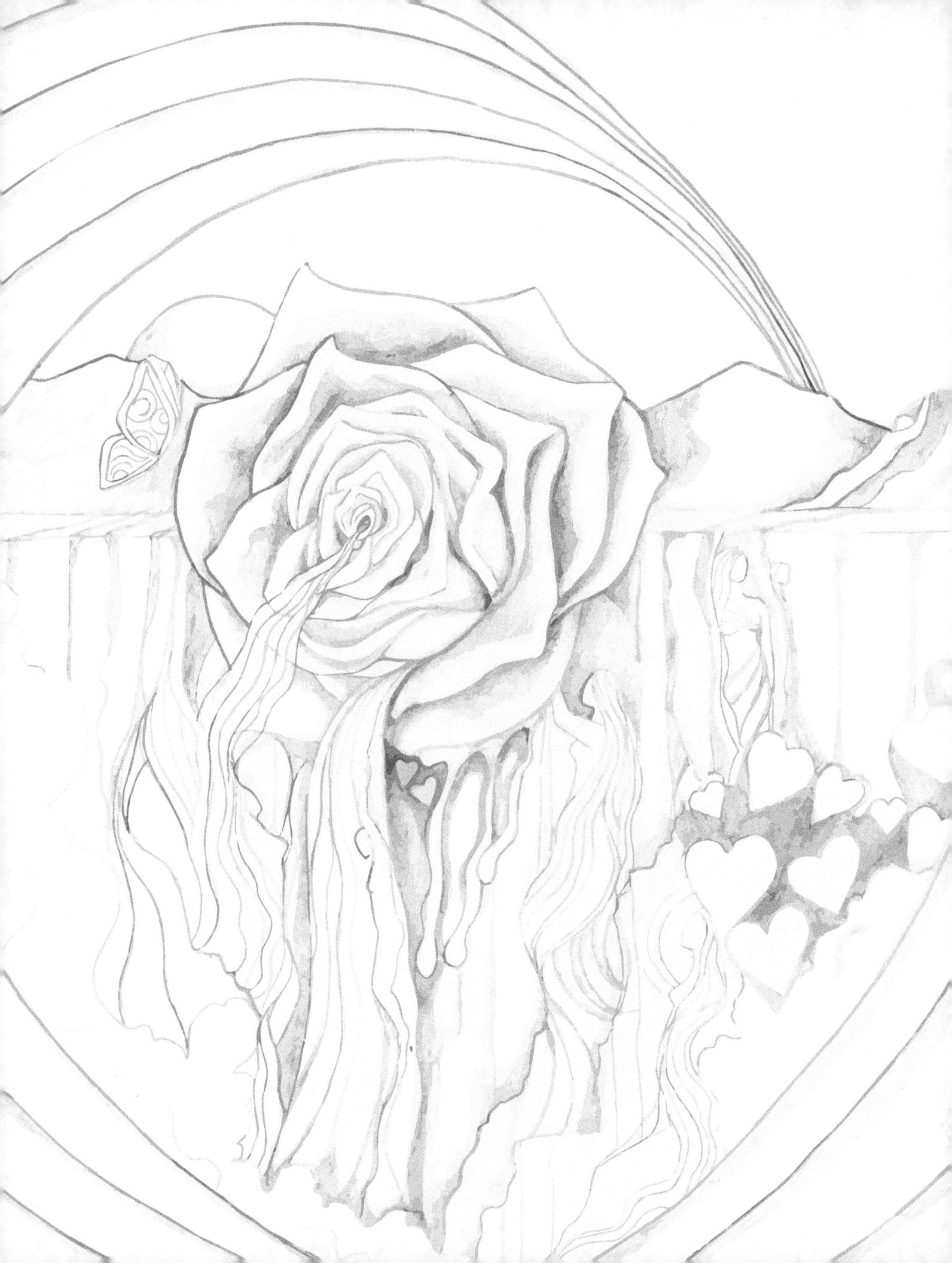

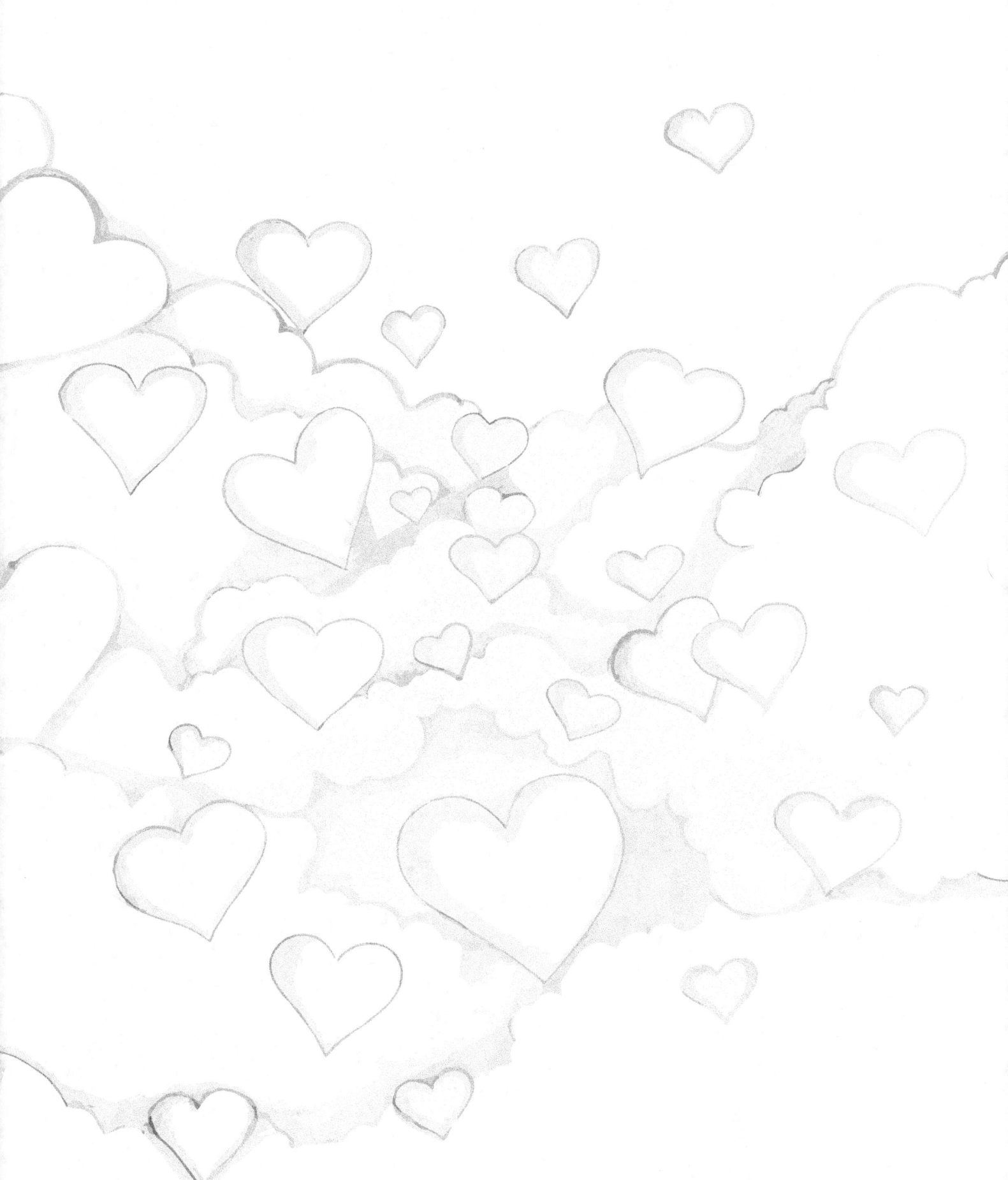

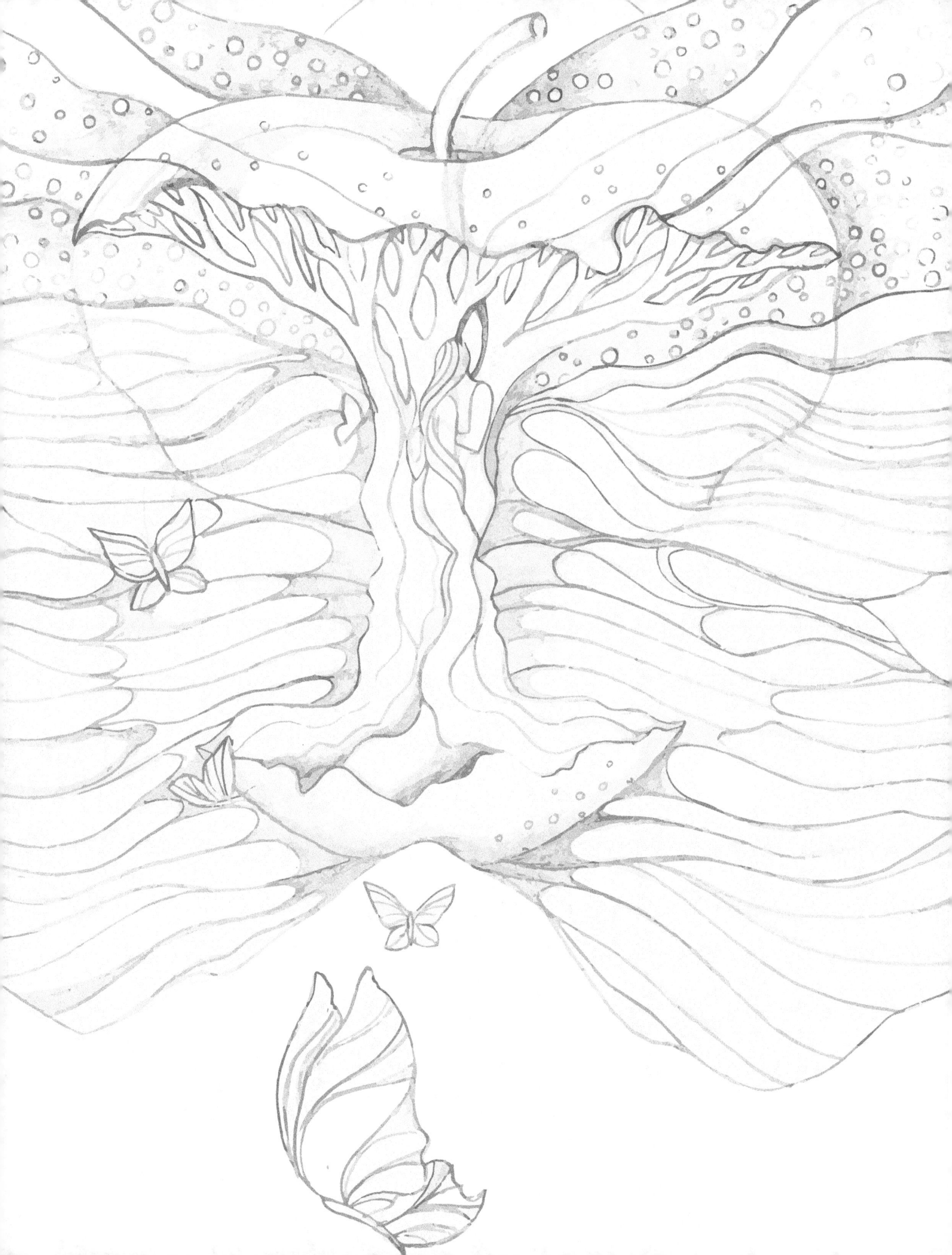

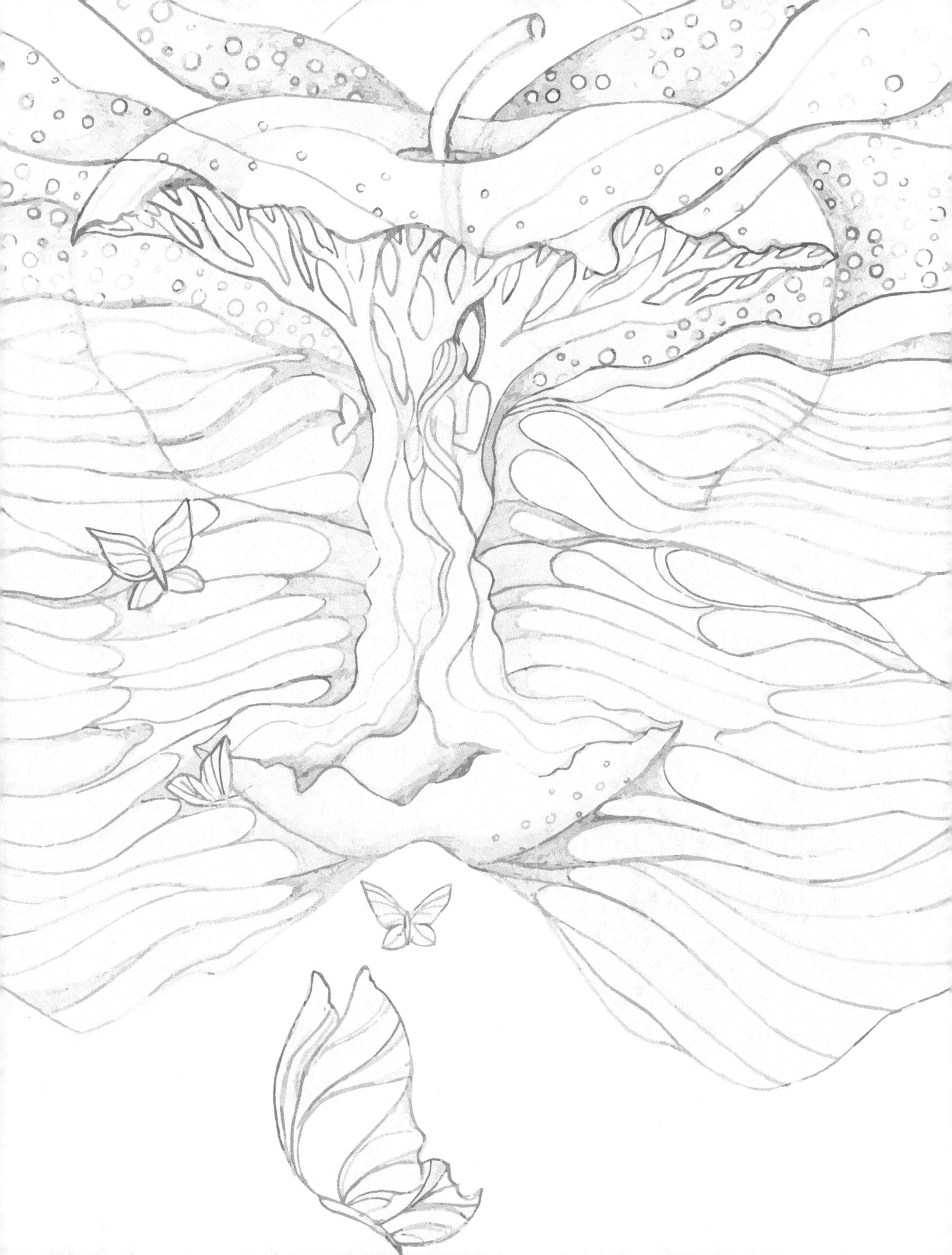

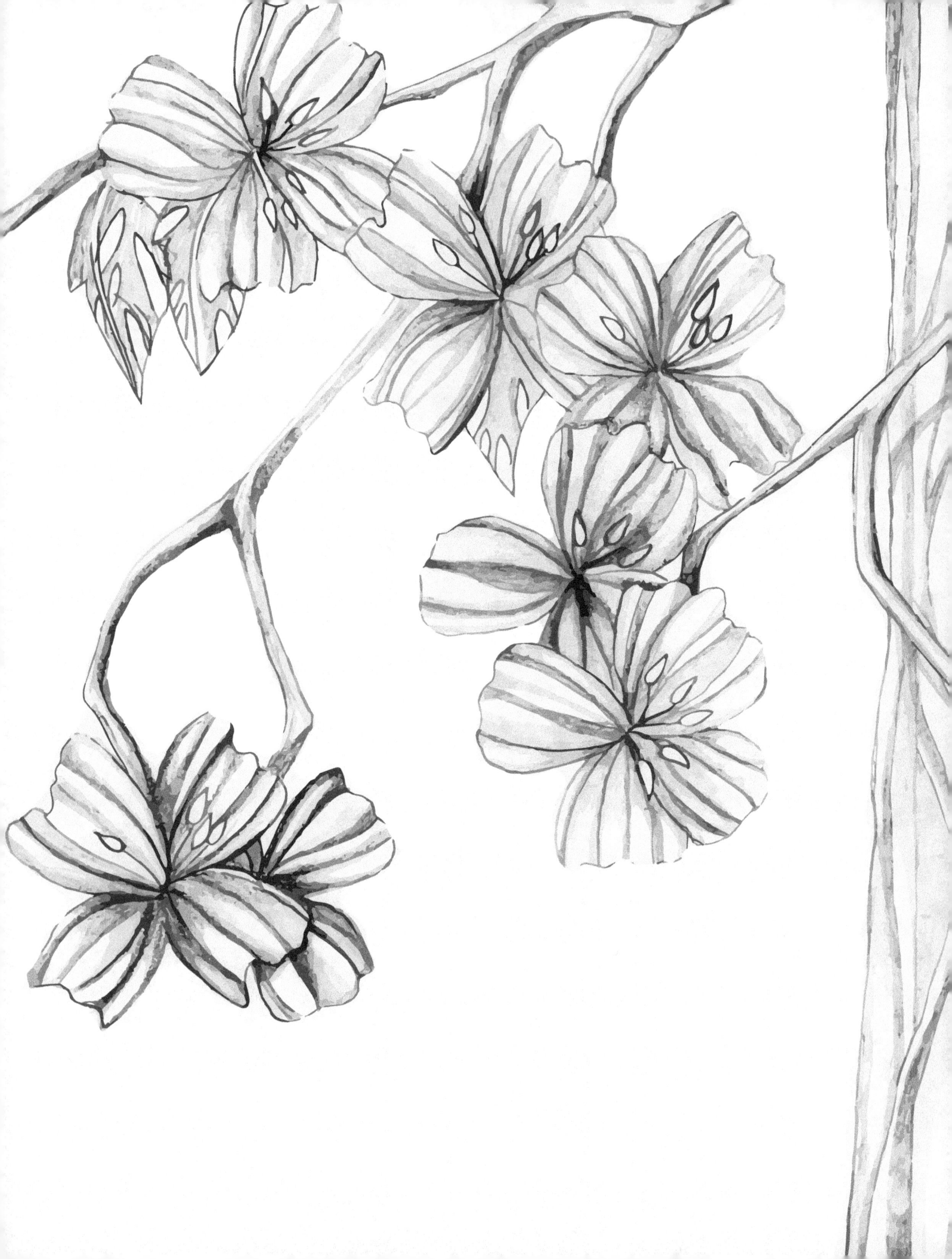

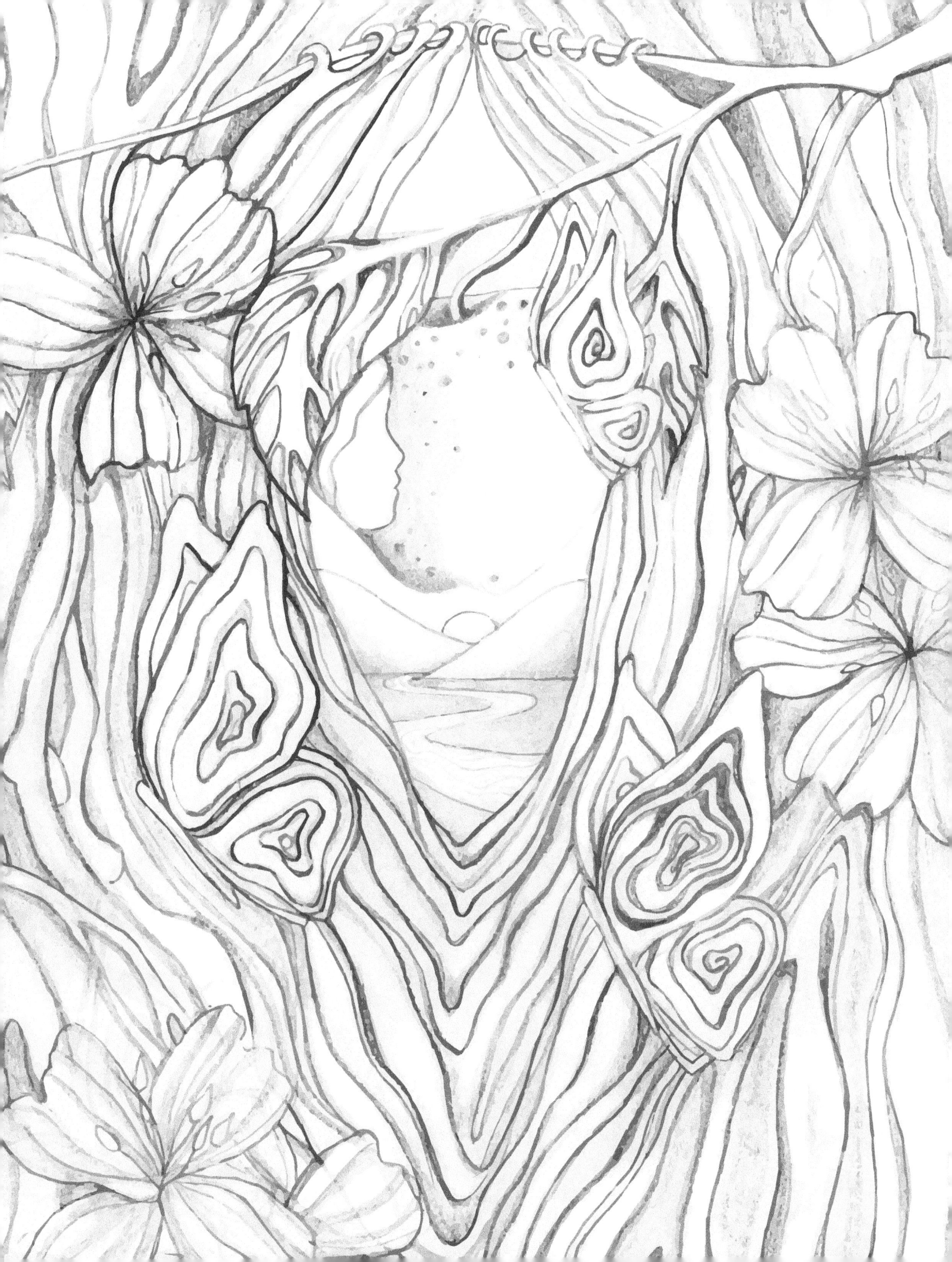

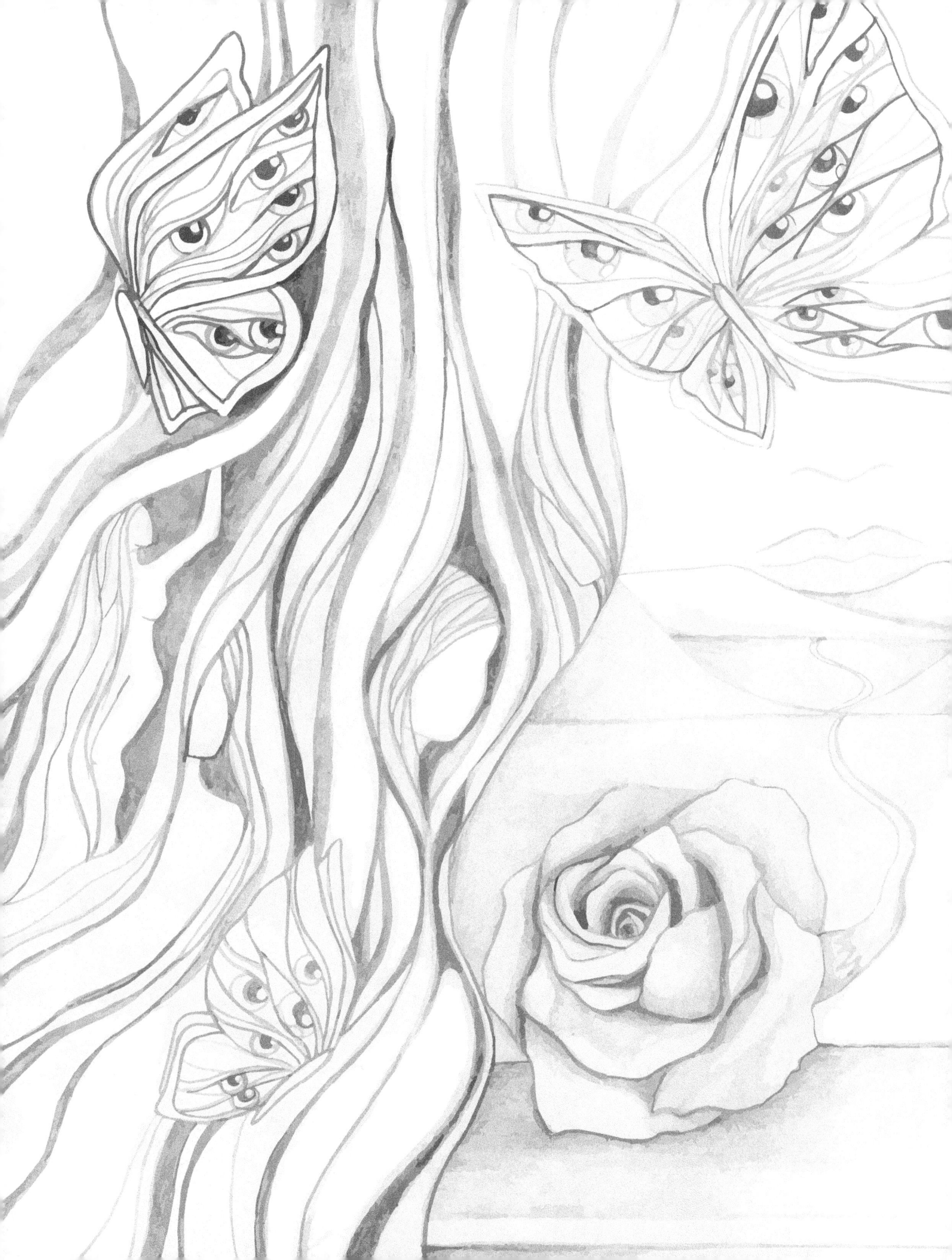

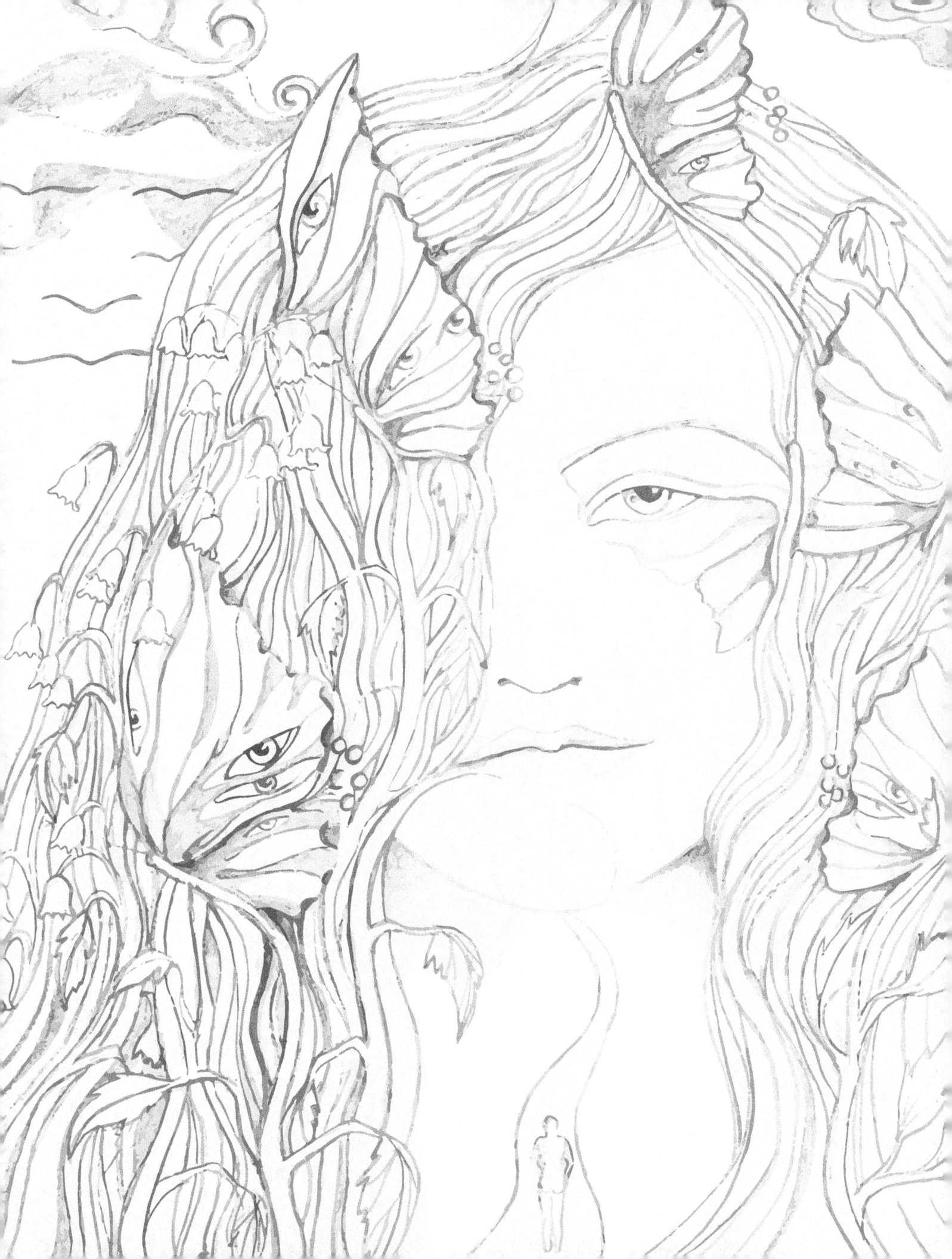

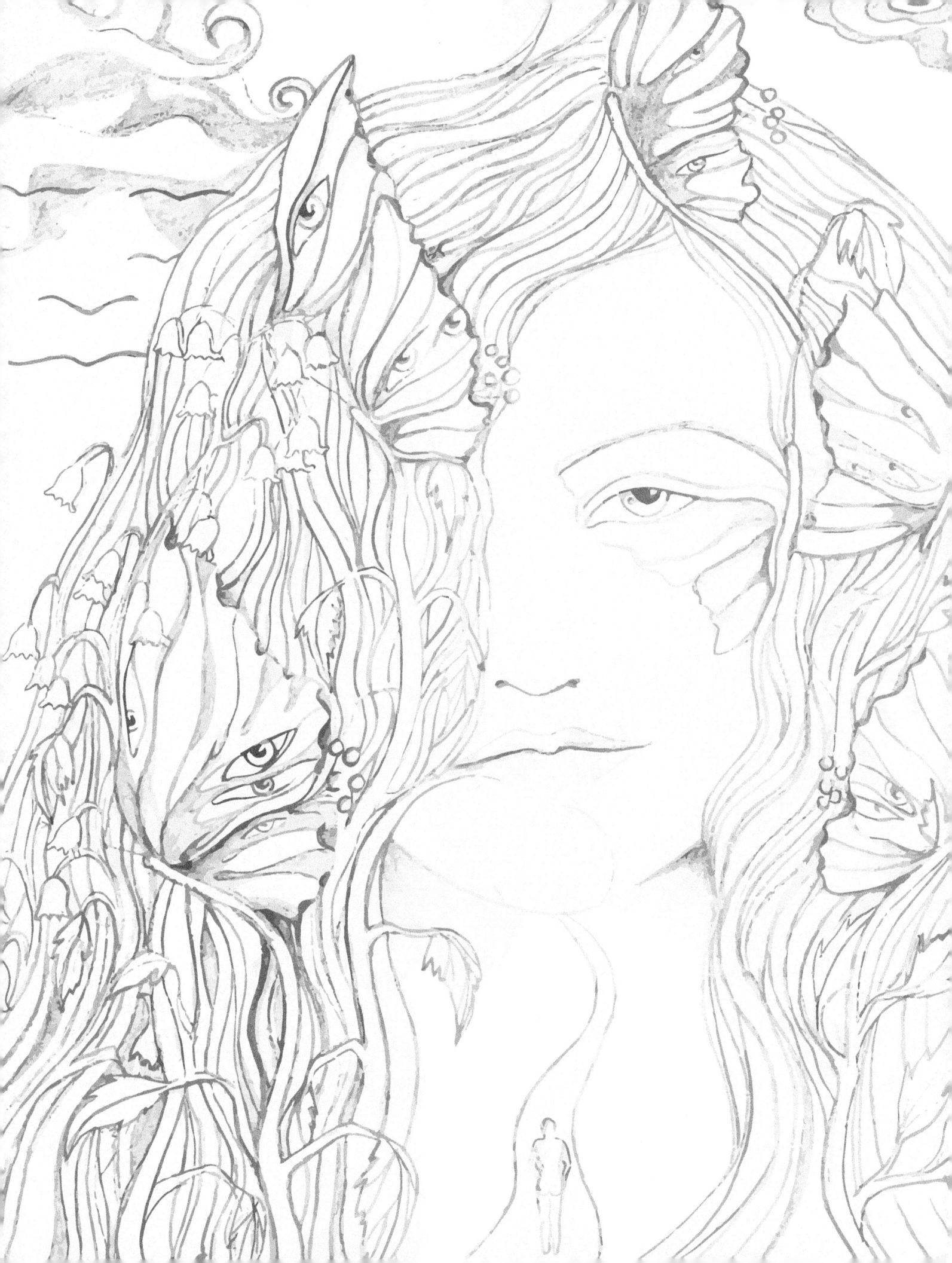

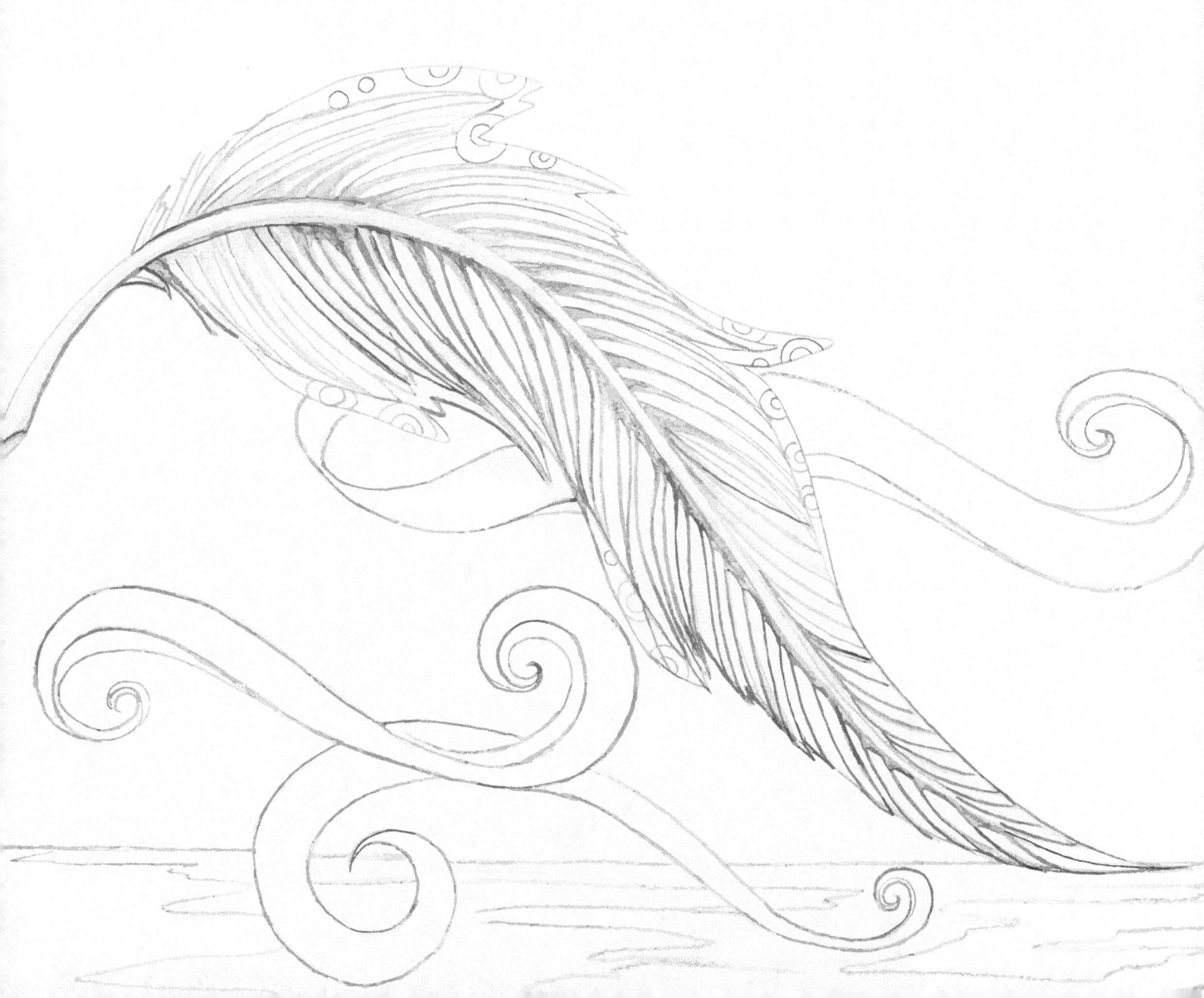

www.serenadaugette.com
www.facebook.com/serenadaugetteart